Dash Diet Cookbook for Beginners

Table of Contents

Introduction 8

Chapter 1 4 Weeks Meal Plan 11

Chapter 2 Breakfast 13

    1. Baking Powder Biscuits 13

    2. Oatmeal Banana Pancakes with Walnuts 13

    3. Creamy Oats, Greens & Blueberry Smoothie 14

    4. Flaxseed & Banana Smoothie 14

    5. Fruity Tofu Smoothie 14

    6. Cereal with Cranberry-Orange Twist 15

    7. No-Cook Overnight Oats 15

    8. Sweet Potatoes with Coconut Flakes 16

    9. Avocado Cup with Egg 16

    10. Spinach, Egg, and Cheese Breakfast Quesadillas 17

Chapter 3 Vegan Dishes 18

    11. White Bean and Roasted Red Pepper Soup 18

    12. Tomato-Avocado Soup 18

    13. Red Lentil Stew 19

    14. Pasta Primavera 19

    15. Penne with White Beans and Roasted Tomato Sauce 20

    16. Chickpea Burgers 21

    17. Herbed Mushroom Rice 21

    18. Tofu Scramble with Potatoes and Mushrooms 22

    19. Spicy Bean Chili 22

    20. Mexican Beans and Rice 23

Chapter 4 Side Dishes 25

    21. Tomatoes Side Salad 25

22.	Squash Salsa	25
23.	. Apples and Fennel Mix	25
24.	Simple Roasted Celery Mix	26
25.	Thyme Spring Onions	26
26.	Carrot Slaw	27
27.	Watermelon Tomato Salsa	27
28.	Sprouts Side Salad	27
29.	Zucchini and Brussels Sprouts Salad	28
30.	Cabbage Slaw	28

Chapter 5 Vegetarian Dishes 30

31.	Southwestern Bean-And-Pepper Salad	30
32.	Cauliflower Mashed "Potatoes"	30
33.	Roasted Brussels Sprouts	31
34.	Broccoli with Garlic and Lemon	31
35.	Brown-Rice Pilaf	32
36.	Chunky Black-Bean Dip	32
37.	Classic Hummus	33
38.	Crispy Potato Skins	33
39.	Roasted Chickpeas	34
40.	Carrot-Cake Smoothie	34

Chapter 6 Desserts 36

41.	Hearty Cashew and Almond butter	36
42.	The Refreshing Nutter	36
43.	Elegant Cranberry Muffins	36
44.	Cinnamon Ice Cream	37
45.	Stylish Chocolate Parfait	38
46.	Supreme Matcha Bomb	38
47.	Mesmerizing Avocado and Chocolate Pudding	38

DASH DIET COOKBOOK FOR BEGINNERS

1500 DAYS OF DELICIOUS AND LOW SODIUM RECIPES WITH 30-DAYS MEAL PLAN TO LOWER YOUR BLOOD PRESSURE & LIVE HEALTHIER

WRITTEN BY:

ABIGAIL WHITE

© **Copyright 2023 - All rights reserved.**

The content contained within this book may not be reproduced, duplicated or transmitted without direct written permission from the author or the publisher.

Under no circumstances will any blame or legal responsibility be held against the publisher, or author, for any damages, reparation, or monetary loss due to the information contained within this book. Either directly or indirectly.

Legal Notice:

This book is copyright protected. This book is only for personal use. You cannot amend, distribute, sell, use, quote or paraphrase any part, or the content within this book, without the consent of the author or publisher.

Disclaimer Notice:

Please note the information contained within this document is for educational and entertainment purposes only. All effort has been executed to present accurate, up to date, and reliable, complete information. No warranties of any kind are declared or implied. Readers acknowledge that the author is not engaging in the rendering of legal, financial, medical or professional advice. The content within this book has been derived from various sources. Please consult a licensed professional before attempting any techniques outlined in this book.

BY READING THIS DOCUMENT, THE READER AGREES THAT UNDER NO CIRCUMSTANCES IS THE AUTHOR RESPONSIBLE FOR ANY LOSSES, DIRECT OR INDIRECT, WHICH ARE INCURRED AS A RESULT OF THE USE OF INFORMATION CONTAINED WITHIN THIS DOCUMENT, INCLUDING, BUT NOT LIMITED TO, ERRORS, OMISSIONS, OR INACCURACIES.

48. Hearty Pineapple Pudding 39

49. Healthy Berry Cobbler 39

50. Tasty Poached Apples 40

Chapter 7 Beef and Pork 41

51. Decent Beef and Onion Stew 41

52. Zucchini Beef Sauté with Coriander Greens 41

53. Beef Soup 42

54. Almond Butter Pork Chops 42

55. Hearty Pork Belly Casserole 42

56. Healthy Avocado Beef Patties 43

57. Ravaging Beef Pot Roast 43

58. Crazy Japanese Potato and Beef Croquettes 44

59. Cool Cabbage Fried Beef 44

60. Pork, White Bean, and Spinach Soup 45

Chapter 8 Soups 46

61. Curried Kabocha Squash Soup 46

62. Kale and Potato Soup Straight From Ireland 46

63. Potato and Carrot "Impeccable" Soup 47

64. Meticulous Butternut Squash Soup 47

65. "Split" Pea and Sundried Tomatoes Soup 48

66. House's Special Cashew Spring Green Soup 48

67. Omnipotent Organic Chicken Thigh Soup 49

68. Very Low Carb Ham and Cabbage Bowl 49

69. Cabbage and Leek Soup 50

70. Quinoa and Lentil Soup 50

Chapter 9 Fish and Seafood 52

71. Tilapia Tacos with Chipotle Cream 52

72. Baked Haddock with Peppers & Eggplant 52

- 73. Tex-Mex Cod with Roasted Peppers & Corn 53
- 74. Marinated Lime Grilled Shrimp 54
- 75. Shrimp & Broccoli with Angel Hair 54
- 76. Saucy Penne with Shrimp, Peas & Walnuts 55
- 77. Angel Hair with Smoked Salmon & Asparagus 56
- 78. Bass with Citrus Butter 56
- 79. Seared Mahi-Mahi with Lemon & Parsley 57
- 80. Maple-Glazed Salmon 57

Chapter 10 Salads 59

- 81. Southwest Corn and Black Bean Salad 59
- 82. Curried Chicken Salad 59
- 83. Chinese Chicken Salad 60
- 84. Turkey Salad with Apples and Dried Cranberries 60
- 85. Shrimp, Mango, and Black Bean Salad 60
- 86. Tuna and Vegetable Salad 61
- 87. Couscous Salad with Vinaigrette 61
- 88. California Cobb Salad 62
- 89. Chopped Greek Salad 62
- 90. Balsamic Beet Salad 62

Chapter 11 Poultry 64

- 91. Thai Chicken Pasta 64
- 92. Paprika Baked Chicken Breasts 64
- 93. Chicken Lettuce Wraps 65
- 94. Chicken Pita Sandwiches 65
- 95. White Wine Garlic Chicken 66
- 96. Turkey Medallions 66
- 97. Walnut Pesto Chicken Penne 67
- 98. Instant Pot Chicken Thighs with Olives and Capers 67

99.	Instant pot Mediterranean Chicken	68
100.	Green Chicken and Rice Bowl	68

Chapter 12 Snacks 70

101.	Avocado Wedges	70
102.	Lemon Dip	70
103.	Sweet Potato Dip	70
104.	Beans Salsa	71
105.	Green Beans Salsa	71
106.	Delicious Berry Pie	72
107.	Carrot Spread	72
108.	Tomato Dip	72
109.	Salmon Bowls	73
110.	Tomato and Corn Salsa	73

Chapter 13 Dressings, Sauces & Condiments 74

111.	Avocado Dressing	74
112.	Barbeque Sauce	74
113.	Chicken Broth	75
114.	French Dressing	75
115.	Italian Dressing	75
116.	Marinara Sauce	76
117.	Peanut Butter	76
118.	Ranch Dressing	76
119.	Soy Sauce	77
120.	Tartar Sauce	77

Conclusion 79

Introduction

DASH advocates for much less fat than you'd find in a typical American diet. This means that it's lower in calories. This diet eliminates and reduces unhealthy fats, fast food, fried foods, as well as highly processed foods. Instead, it emphasizes healthy fats like omega-3, which are good for your body and help weight loss. These are mostly present in foods with lower calories. The high fiber content in most of the foods recommended under the DASH diet is another great contributor to weight loss because fibers help you have a feeling of satiety while also aiding digestion so your body. At the same time, it can eliminate wastes while slowing down the absorption of sugar and fat. This promotes efficient regulation and response to insulin, limiting the risk of and symptoms of metabolic syndrome.

Now that you know a little more about the DASH Diet and its benefits, it's time to talk about food! Starting from the top, I'll share with you exactly what kinds of foods you can eat and the serving size, along with what you should avoid or limit.

Vegetables

Vegetables are packed with magnesium, potassium, as well as healthy vitamins and fibers, so it's no wonder they're all welcomed on the DASH Diet. This includes raw, cooked, fresh, or frozen vegetables.

Your goal is to have 4-5 servings per day. An example of 1 serving is 1 cup of raw salad greens or 1/2 cup of chopped-up veggies.

Fruits

Fruits are not only easy to enjoy as a snack, side dish, or for breakfast, they're rich in fiber, potassium, and magnesium.

You'll need to eat 4-5 servings of fruit per day on the Dash Diet. An example of 1 serving is a medium-sized fruit or ½ cup of fresh, frozen, or canned fruit.

Low-Fat or Fat-Free Dairy

While you're on the DASH Diet, you'll need to aim for low-fat or fat-free dairy products.

On the DASH Diet, you can have 2-3 servings of dairy per day; 1 serving is 1 cup of 1% milk or low-fat yogurt.

Whole-Grains

When it comes to grains on the DASH Diet, whole grains are preferred over very refined grains. That's mainly because whole grains have far more nutrients and fiber, while processed grains are stripped of their dietary fiber, iron, and many B vitamins.

You can enjoy 7-8 servings of whole-grain products per day. An example of 1 serving is 1 slice of bread or 1/2 cup of pasta or rice.

Lean Meat, Fish, and Poultry

On the diet, you can have 6 servings/ounces per day or less. An example of 1 serving is the area of your palm covered with 3 ounces of meat.

Seeds and Legumes

Seeds and legumes are allowed because they are such a good source of protein, potassium, and magnesium. They also contain antioxidants that protect against certain types of cancer and cardiovascular disease.

On the DASH Diet, you can have 4-5 servings of nuts, seeds, and legumes per week. An example of 1 serving is 2 tbsp. of sunflower seeds or 1/3 cup of nuts.

Also, please note that these servings are based on a 2,000-calorie diet, so you may have to consume more or less than 2,000 calories a day depending on your gender, age, and activity level.

Food to Eat

Vegetables	Asparagus, artichokes, cabbage, mushrooms, bell peppers, cauliflower, beets, lettuce, onions, celery, broccoli, parsnips, Brussels sprouts, eggplants, and corn.
Fruit	Apples, pineapples, blueberries, dates, kiwi fruit, papaya, mango, cherries, pears, apricots, plums, peaches, strawberries, honeydew, lemons, bananas, grapefruit, prunes, blackberries, and tangerines.
Non-fat or low-fat dairy	Greek yogurt, low-fat sour cream, feta cottage cheese, low-fat buttermilk, mozzarella (part-skim), chevre (goat cheese), soft parmesan cheese, low fat or fat-free milk, trans-fat-free kefir, reduced-fat cheddar, Monterey jack.
Lean proteins	Fish fillets (plain), salmon, deli meat, turkey (skinless), chicken (ground, lean), shrimp, tofu, eggs, tempeh, beef: sirloin, round or flank and lean, pork.
Whole grains	Whole-wheat pasta, quinoa, amaranth, spelt, barley, wild rice, couscous, triticale, bulgur, kasha (buckwheat), millet, oats (old fashioned), and brown rice.
Healthy snacks	Bean-based spreads like black bean dip or hummus, raw veggie sticks and raw unsalted nuts, dried fruit popcorn, whole-grain pretzels, whole-grain crackers.
Nuts and seeds	Walnuts, sunflower seeds, pumpkin seeds, hazelnuts, cashews, almonds, nut butter.
Beverages	Sparkling water, herbal tea, low-sodium vegetable juice, 100% fruit juice, low-sodium broth.

Foods to Avoid

The foods and drinks you should avoid while following the dash diet include foods high in salt and sugar as well as high-fat snacks such as:

- Canned soups
- Sauces and gravies
- White Bread and rolls
- Cured meats and cold cuts
- Processed Cheese
- Salad dressings
- Red meat that is not grass-fed
- Pastries
- Sugary beverages
- Sodas
- Salted nuts
- Potato Chips
- Cookies
- Candy

With that information on the foods to eat and those to avoid, let us now learn how you can actually adopt the DASH diet.

Chapter 1
4 Weeks Meal Plan

DAY	BREAKFAST	LUNCH	DINNER
1	BAKING POWDER BISCUIT	ORANGE JUICE SMOOTHIE	FAJITA CHLLI
2	FLAXSEED&BANANA PANCAKE	MINTED PEAS FETA RICE	TURKEY BARLEY SOUP
3	NO COOK OVERNIGHT OATS	HEARTHY BABY CARROT	CHERRY CHICKEN WRAPS
4	AVOCADO CUP WITH EGG	SENSITIVE STEAMED ARTICHOKES	WALNUT PESTO CHICKEN PENNE
5	METIRRANEAN TOAST	ZUCCHINI CAKE	TURKEY AND PEACH
6	APPLE PANCAKE	POPOVERS	BALSAMIC CHICKEN
7	BUCKWHEAT CREPES	VEGAN RICE PUDDING	CREAMY TURKEY MIX
8	INSTANT BANANA OATMEAL	CINNAMON SCENTED QUINOA	TURKEY MEDALLIONS
9	SIMPLE CHEESE AND BROCCOLI OMELETS	GREEN VEGETABLE SMOOTHIE	WHITE WINE GARLIC CHICKEN
10	BLUEBERRY WAFFLE	TOMATES SIDE SALAD	THIA CHICKEN PASTA
11	VANILLA TOAST	SQUASH SALSA	CARROT SOUP WITH CURRY
12	APPLE OATS	APPLES AND FENNEL MIX	CREAMY ASPARAGUS SOUP
13	BAGELS MADE HEALTHY	SIMPLE ROASTED CELERY MIX	PUMPKIN SOUP IN COCONUT MILK
14	SAVORY YOGURT BOWLS	THYME SPRING ONIONS	LEEK & CAULIFLOWER SOUP
15	ENERGY SUNRISE MUFFINS	CARROT SLAW	CARROT SOUP WITH CURRY
16	GRANOLA PARFAIT	WATERMELON TOMATOES SALSA	GARLIC VEGGIE SOUP
17	WHOLE GRAIN PANCAKE	ZUCCHINI AND BRUSSELS SPROUTS SALAD	ONION SOUP
18	BREAK HASH	CABBAGE SLAW	FRESH PARFIAT
19	FRUIT SCONES	CAULIFLOWER RISOTTO	DEICIOUS PEACH PIE
20	SUPER SIMPLE GRANOLA	THREE BENS MIX	SIMPLE BROWNIES
21	SALSA EGGS	SPICED BROCCOLI FLORETS	APPLE TART
22	BEAN FRITTATA	BUTTER CORN	EASY CHOCOLATE CAKE
23	EGG TOAST	CREAMY CUCUMBER MIX	EASY FUDGE
24	ASPARAGUS OMELETS	SWEET BUTTERNUT	FRUIT SALAD
25	RASPBERRY YOGURT	BELL PEPERS MIX	BANANA CAKE
26	PEACH PANCAKES	FLAVOURED TURNIPS MIX	CHOCOLATE PUDDING

DAY	BREAKFAST	LUNCH	DINNER
27	RED BEAN AND RICE	LIMA BEANS DISH	COCONUT MOUSSE
28	SOUTHWEST TOFU SCRAMBLES	SOUR CREAM GREEN BEANS	MANGO PUDDING
29	AVOCADO EGG TOAST	PEACH AND CARROTS	FRUIT SKEWERS
30	SPICED PEPPER RELISH	MARINARA SAUCE	CHICKEN BROTH

DAY	BREAKFAST	LUNCH	DINNER

Chapter 2
Breakfast

1. Baking Powder Biscuits

Preparation time: 5 minutes

Cooking time: 5 minutes

Servings: 1

- 4 tbsp. Non-hydrogenated vegetable shortening
- 1 tbsp. sugar
- 2/3 c. low-
- Fat milk
- 1 c. unbleached all-purpose flour
- 4 tsp.
- Sodium-free baking powder

Ingredients:

- 1 egg white
- 1 c. white whole-wheat flour

Directions:

1. Preheat oven to 450°F. Take out a baking sheet and set it aside.
2. Place the flour, sugar, and baking powder into a mixing bowl and whisk well to combine.
3. Cut the shortening into the mixture using your fingers, and work until it resembles coarse crumbs. Add the egg white and milk and stir to combine.
4. Turn the dough out onto a lightly floured surface and knead for 1 minute. Roll dough to ¾ inch thickness and cut into 12 rounds.
5. Place rounds on the baking sheet. Place baking sheet on middle rack in the oven and bake 10 minutes.
6. Remove baking sheet and place biscuits on a wire rack to cool.

Nutrition:

- Calories: 118
- Fat: 4 g
- Carbs: 16 g
- Protein: 3 g
- Sugars: 0.2 g
- Sodium: 6 %

2. Oatmeal Banana Pancakes with Walnuts

Preparation time: 15 minutes

Cooking time: 5 minutes

Servings: 8 pancakes

Ingredients:

- 1 finely diced firm banana
- 1 c. whole wheat pancake mix
- 1/8 c. chopped walnuts
- 1/4 c. old-fashioned oats

Directions:

1. Make the pancake mix according to the directions on the package.
2. Add walnuts, oats, and chopped bananas.
3. Coat a griddle with cooking spray. Add about ¼ cup of the pancake batter onto the griddle when hot.
4. Turn pancake over when bubbles form on top. Cook until golden brown.
5. Serve immediately.

Nutrition:

- Calories: 155
- Fat: 4 g
- Carbs: 28 g
- Protein: 7 g
- Sugars: 2.2 g
- Sodium: 16 %

3. Creamy Oats, Greens & Blueberry Smoothie

Preparation time: 4 minutes **Servings:** 1

Cooking time: 0 minutes

Ingredients:

- 1 c. cold
- Fat-free milk
- 1 c. salad greens
- ½ c. fresh frozen blueberries
- ½ c. frozen cooked oatmeal
- 1 tbsp. sunflower seeds

Directions:

1. In a powerful blender, blend all ingredients until smooth and creamy.
2. Serve and enjoy.

Nutrition:

- Calories: 280
- Fat: 6.8 g
- Carbs: 44.0 g
- Protein: 14.0 g
- Sugars: 32 g
- Sodium: 141 %

4. Flaxseed & Banana Smoothie

Preparation time: 5 minutes **Servings:** 1

Cooking time: 0 minutes

Ingredients:

- 1 frozen banana ½ c. almond milk
- Vanilla extract. 1 tbsp. almond butter
- 2 tbsp. flax seed 1 tsp. maple syrup

Directions:

- Add all your ingredients to a food processor or blender and run until smooth. Pour the mixture into a glass and enjoy.

Nutrition:

- Calories: 376
- Fat: 19.4 g
- Carbs: 48.3 g
- Protein: 9.2 g
- Sugars: 12 %
- Sodium: 64.9 mg

5. Fruity Tofu Smoothie

Preparation time: 5 minutes

Cooking time: 0 minutes

Servings: 2

Ingredients:

- 1 c. ice cold water
- 1 c. packed spinach
- ¼ c. frozen mango chunks
- ½ c. frozen pineapple chunks
- 1 tbsp. chia seeds
- 1 container silken tofu
- 1 frozen medium banana

Directions:

1. In a powerful blender, add all ingredients and puree until smooth and creamy.
2. Evenly divide into two glasses, serve and enjoy.

Nutrition:

- Calories: 175
- Fat: 3.7 g
- Carbs: 33.3 g
- Protein: 6.0 g
- Sugars: 16.3 g
- Sodium: 1 %

6. Cereal with Cranberry-Orange Twist

Preparation time: 5 minutes

Cooking time: 0 minutes

Servings: 1

Ingredients:

- ½ c. water
- ½ c. orange juice
- 1/3 c. oat bran
- ¼ c. dried cranberries
- Sugar
- Milk

Directions:

1. In a bowl, combine all ingredients.
2. For about 2 minutes, microwave the bowl, then serve with sugar and milk.
3. Enjoy!

Nutrition:

- Calories: 220.4
- Fat: 2.4 g
- Carbs: 43.5 g
- Protein: 6.2 g
- Sugars: 8 g
- Sodium: 1%

7. No-Cook Overnight Oats

Preparation time: 5 minutes

Cooking time: 0 minutes

Servings: 1

Ingredients:

- 1 1/2 c. low fat milk
- 5 whole almond pieces
- 1 tsp. chia seeds
- 2 tbsp. oats
- 1 tsp. sunflower seeds
- 1 tbsp. raisins

Directions:

1. In a jar or mason bottle with the cap, mix all ingredients.

2. Refrigerate overnight.
3. Enjoy for breakfast. Will keep in the fridge for up to 3 days.

Nutrition:

- Calories: 271
- Fat: 9.8 g
- Carbs: 35.4 g
- Protein: 16.7 g
- Sugars: 9 g
- Sodium: 103 %

8. Sweet Potatoes with Coconut Flakes

Preparation time: 15 minutes

Servings: 2

Cooking time: 1 hour

Ingredients:

- 16 oz. sweet potatoes
- 1 tbsp. maple syrup
- ¼ c. fat-free coconut
- Greek yogurt
- 1/8 c. unsweetened toasted coconut flakes
- 1 chopped apple

Directions:

1. Preheat oven to 400°F.
2. Place your potatoes on a baking sheet. Bake them for 45 - 60 minutes or until soft.
3. Use a sharp knife to mark "X" on the potatoes and fluff pulp with a fork.
4. Top with coconut flakes, chopped apple, Greek yogurt, and maple syrup.
5. Serve immediately.

Nutrition:

- Calories: 321
- Fat: 3 g
- Carbs: 70 g
- Protein: 7 g
- Sugars: 0.1 g
- Sodium: 3 %

9. Avocado Cup with Egg

Preparation time: 5 minutes

Servings: 4

Cooking time: 30 minutes

Ingredients:

- 4 tsp. parmesan cheese
- 1 chopped stalk scallion
- 4 dashes pepper
- 4 dashes paprika
- 2 ripe avocados
- 4 medium eggs

Directions:

1. Preheat oven to 375°F.
2. Slice avocadoes in half and discard the seed.
3. Slice the avocado's rounded portions, make it level, and sit well on a baking sheet.
4. Place avocadoes on a baking sheet and crack one egg in each hole of the avocado.
5. Season each egg evenly with pepper and paprika.
6. Pop in the oven and bake for 25 minutes or until eggs are cooked to your liking.
7. Serve with a sprinkle of parmesan.

Nutrition:

- Calories: 206
- Fat: 15.4 g
- Carbs: 11.3 g
- Protein: 8.5 g
- Sugars: 0.4 g
- Sodium: 21 %

10. Spinach, Egg, and Cheese Breakfast Quesadillas

Preparation time: 10 minutes

Cooking time: 15 minutes

Servings: 4

Ingredients:

- 1½ tbsp. extra-virgin olive oil
- ½ medium onion, diced
- 1 medium red bell pepper, diced 4 large eggs
- 1/8 tsp. salt
- 1/8 tsp. freshly ground black pepper 4 cups baby spinach
- ½ cup crumbled feta cheese
- Nonstick cooking spray
- 4 (6-inch) whole-wheat tortillas, divided
- 1 cup shredded part-skim low-moisture mozzarella cheese, divided

Directions:

1. In a large skillet, heat the oil over medium heat. Add the onion and bell pepper and sauté for about 5 minutes, or until soft.
2. In a medium bowl, whisk together the eggs, salt, and black pepper. Stir spinach and feta cheese. Add the egg mixture to the skillet and scramble for about 2 minutes, or until the eggs are cooked. Remove from the heat.
3. Coat a clean skillet with cooking spray and add 2 tortillas. Put one squinch of the spinach-egg mixture on one side of each tortilla. Sprinkle each w cup of mozzarella cheese. Fold the other halves of the tortillas down to the quesadillas and brown for about 1 minute. Flip and cook for another minute on the other side. Repeat with the remaining 2 tortillas and ½ cup mozzarella cheese.
4. Cut each quesadilla in half or wedges. Divide among 4 storage container reusable bags.

Nutrition:

- Calories: 453
- Total Fat: 28 g
- Carbs: 28 g
- Fiber: 4.5 g
- Protein: 23 g
- Calcium: 394 mg
- Vitamin D: 45 IU
- Potassium: 205 mg
- Magnesium: 59 mg
- Sodium: 837 mg

Chapter 3
Vegan Dishes

11. White Bean and Roasted Red Pepper Soup

Preparation Time: 10 minutes

Cooking Time: 45 minutes

Serving: 4

- 1 tbsp. olive oil
- 1 small onion, chopped
- 1/8 tsp. crushed red pepper
- 2 cups low-sodium vegetable broth
- 2 cups water
- 1 (15-ounce) can cannellini (white kidney) beans, drained and rinsed

Ingredients:

- 3 large red bell peppers

Direction:

1. Preheat the broiler to high. Place the bell peppers on a baking sheet. Broil, turning peppers frequently until sides are blistered and charred. Remove from broiler.
2. Carefully place peppers in a plastic or paper bag; let stand 20 minutes. Peel off the layer of skin, and remove the core and seeds.
3. Heat the olive oil in a large skillet over medium-high heat. Add the onion. Cook, occasionally stirring, for 3 to 5 minutes, or until the onions are tender.
4. Add the roasted peppers and crushed red pepper and cook for 1 minute.
5. Stir in the broth, water, and beans. Bring to a boil. Reduce the heat to low, and cook for 5 minutes.
6. Serve immediately.

Nutrition:

- Calories: 169
- Total Fat: 5 g
- Saturated Fat: 1 g
- Cholesterol: 0 mg
- Sodium: 180 mg
- Potassium: 196 mg
- Magnesium: 66 mg
- Total Carbs: 26 g
- Fiber: 8 g
- Sugars: 4 g
- Protein: 7 g

12. Tomato-Avocado Soup

Preparation Time: 5 minutes

Cooking Time: 12 minutes

Serving: 4

Ingredients:

- 1/2 tbsp. olive oil
- 1 cup chopped onion

- 1 clove garlic, minced
- 1 (14.5-ounce) can no-salt diced tomatoes in juice
- 1 cup low-sodium vegetable broth
- 1 cup water
- 1/2 tsp. freshly ground black pepper
- 1 cup low-fat buttermilk
- 1 large ripe avocado, halved, pitted, peeled, and sliced

Directions:

1. Heat the olive oil in a large pot over medium heat. Add the onion, and cook, frequently stirring, about 5 minutes, or until translucent. Add the garlic, and cook for 1 minute.
2. Transfer the onion-and-garlic mixture to a blender. Add the tomatoes and juice, broth, water, black pepper, and purée until smooth.
3. Transfer the purée back to the pot and heat the soup mixture over medium-low heat for 5 minutes or until heated through. Add the buttermilk, and stir to combine.
4. Garnish each serving with a quarter of the avocado slices.

Nutrition:

- Calories: 155
- Total Fat: 9 g
- Saturated Fat: 2 g
- Cholesterol: 3 mg
- Sodium: 116 mg
- Potassium: 653 mg
- Magnesium: 40 mg
- Total Carbs: 17 g
- Fiber: 5 g
- Sugars: 4 g
- Protein: 5 g

13. Red Lentil Stew

Preparation Time: 5 minutes

Cooking Time: 40 minutes

Serving: 4

Ingredients:

- 1 yellow onion, chopped
- 2 garlic cloves, minced
- 1 small bell pepper, chopped
- 3 medium carrots, peeled and chopped
- 1 (14.5-ounce) can no-salt diced tomatoes in juice
- 1 cup dried red lentils, rinsed
- 5 cups low-sodium vegetable broth

Directions:

1. Spray a large pot with nonstick cooking spray and heat over medium heat. Add the onions and garlic and sauté until translucent, about 5 minutes.
2. Add the pepper and carrots, and sauté for 2 to 3 minutes.
3. Add the tomatoes and their juice, lentils, and vegetable broth and bring to a boil.
4. Reduce the heat to low. Cover the pot and simmer for about 30 minutes until the lentils are tender.
5. Ladle the stew into soup bowls and serve.

Nutrition:

- Calories: 197
- Fat: 1 g
- Cholesterol: 0 mg
- Sodium: 222 mg
- Potassium: 889 mg
- Magnesium: 64 mg
- Total Carbs: 38 g
- Fiber: 13 g
- Sugars: 6 g
- Protein: 11 g

14. Pasta Primavera

Preparation Time: 10 minutes

Cooking Time: 15 minutes

Serving: 4

Ingredients:

- 2 cups broccoli florets
- 1 cup sliced mushrooms
- 1 cup sliced zucchini or yellow squash
- 1 tbsp. olive oil, plus 1 tsp.
- 2 garlic cloves, minced
- 3/4 cup fat-free evaporated milk
- 1/2 cup freshly grated Parmesan cheese
- 8 ounces whole-wheat angel hair or spaghetti pasta
- 1/3 cup chopped fresh parsley (optional)

Directions:

1. In a large pot fitted with a steamer basket, bring about 1 inch of water to a boil. Add the broccoli, mushrooms, and zucchini. Cover and steam until tender-crisp, about 10 minutes. Remove from the pot.
2. In a large saucepan, heat 1 tablespoon of the olive oil over medium heat. Add the garlic and sauté over medium heat for 2 to 3 minutes. Add the steamed vegetables and stir or shake to coat the vegetables with the garlic. Remove the saucepan from the heat but keep warm.
3. In another large saucepan, heat the remaining 1 teaspoon olive oil, evaporated milk, and Parmesan cheese. Stir continuously over medium heat until somewhat thickened and heated through without scalding. Remove the saucepan from the heat but keep warm.
4. Fill a large pot three-quarters full with water and bring to a boil. Put the pasta and cook according to the package directions until the desired doneness. Drain the pasta.
5. Divide the pasta evenly among four plates. Top each serving with a quarter of the vegetables and Parmesan sauce. Garnish with fresh parsley (if using) and serve immediately.

Nutrition:

- Calories: 350
- Total Fat: 9 g
- Saturated Fat: 3 g
- Cholesterol: 12 mg
- Sodium: 317 mg
- Potassium: 491 mg
- Magnesium: 44 mg
- Total Carbs: 53 g
- Fiber: 7 g
- Sugars: 7 g
- Protein: 17 g

15. Penne with White Beans and Roasted Tomato Sauce

Preparation Time: 5 minutes

Cooking Time: 25 minutes

Serving: 4

Ingredients:

- 2 pints cherry tomatoes, halved
- 2 tbsp. chopped fresh basil
- 2 tbsp. olive oil, divided
- 8 ounces whole-wheat penne
- 2 garlic cloves, minced
- 1 (15-ounce) can white beans (navy or great northern), drained and rinsed
- 1 tbsp. balsamic vinegar

Directions:

1. On a large sheet pan, toss the tomatoes with the basil and 1 tablespoon of olive oil. Place the pan in the oven and roast until wilted and beginning to brown, about 20 minutes.
2. Meanwhile, cook the penne according to the package directions. Reserve ¼ cup of the cooking water and drain. Add the pasta, beans, tomato mixture, garlic, balsamic vinegar, and the cooking water to a medium pot and simmer for 2 minutes.
3. Drizzle the pasta with the remaining 1 tablespoon of olive oil and serve.

Nutrition:

- Calories: 370
- Total Fat: 9 g
- Saturated Fat: 1 g
- Cholesterol: 0 mg
- Sodium: 121 mg
- Potassium: 317 mg
- Magnesium: 36 mg
- Total Carbs: 66 g
- Fiber: 6 g
- Sugars: 1 g
- Protein: 13 g

16. Chickpea Burgers

Preparation Time: 5 minutes

Cooking Time: 30 minutes

Serving: 4

Ingredients:

- 2 tsp. olive oil
- 1 small yellow onion, diced
- 2 cups rolled oats (not instant)
- ½ cup ground walnuts
- 1 (15-ounce) can chickpeas, drained and rinsed
- 3/4 cup nonfat or low-fat milk
- 1/2 tsp. garlic powder
- 1/2 tsp. onion powder
- 1/2 tsp. dried sage

Directions:

1. In a large skillet, heat the olive oil. Add the onions and cook for about 10 minutes, until very tender and golden brown. Set aside.
2. In a large bowl, toss together the oats and ground walnuts. Set aside.
3. In a blender, combine the chickpeas, milk, garlic powder, onion powder, and dried sage, and process until smooth and creamy.
4. Pour the chickpea mixture into the bowl with the oats and walnuts. Add the browned onions and mix well.
5. Allow the mixture to rest for 5 to 10 minutes, so the oats can absorb the liquid.
6. Form the mixture into eight thin, flat patties. Using the same skillet, brown the burgers over medium-low heat for 5 to 7 minutes on each side.
7. Serve with your favorite toppings.

Nutrition:

- Calories: 375
- Total Fat: 16 g
- Saturated Fat: 1 g
- Cholesterol: 1 mg
- Sodium: 112 mg
- Potassium: 172 mg
- Magnesium: 40 mg
- Total Carbs: 48 g
- Fiber: 11 g
- Sugars: 4 g
- Protein: 14 g

17. Herbed Mushroom Rice

Preparation Time: 10 minutes

Cooking Time: 15 minutes

Serving: 4

Ingredients:

- 2 tsp. olive oil
- 12 ounces sliced mushrooms
- 3 scallion stalks, thinly sliced and separated
- ¾ tsp. freshly ground black pepper
- 2 cups water
- 1 tsp. dried rosemary
- 1 cup dry instant brown rice
- 2 cups frozen lima beans
- ¼ cup shredded Romano cheese (optional)

Direction:

1. Heat the olive oil in a large saucepan over medium-high heat. Add the mushrooms, the white parts of the scallions, and the black pepper and sauté until the mushrooms are just cooked for about 5 minutes.
2. Add the water and rosemary, and bring to a boil over high heat. Stir in the rice, lima beans, and half of the green parts of the scallions, and reduce the heat to medium. Cook, occasionally stirring, for 6 to 8 minutes, or until the rice is done and the lima beans are tender.
3. Sprinkle each serving with cheese (if using) and the remaining green parts of the scallions. Serve immediately.

Nutrition:

- Calories: 220
- Total Fat: 4 g
- Saturated Fat: 0 g
- Cholesterol: 0 mg
- Sodium: 11 mg
- Potassium: 488 mg
- Magnesium: 84 mg
- Total Carbs: 40 g
- Fiber: 9 g
- Sugars: 1 g
- Protein: 10 g

18. Tofu Scramble with Potatoes and Mushrooms

Preparation Time: 10 minutes **Serving:** 4

Cooking Time: 15 minutes

Ingredients:

- 1 large Yukon gold potato, peeled and cut into ½-inch pieces
- 1 tbsp. olive oil
- 1 bunch scallions, thinly sliced
- 2 garlic cloves
- 1 tsp. chili powder
- 1 tsp. cumin
- 2 cups sliced mushrooms
- 1 (14-ounce) block firm tofu, drained and crumbled
- 1 large tomato, sliced or diced (optional)

Directions:

1. Place the potato pieces in a large skillet and cover them with water. Bring to a boil, then reduce the heat to medium and simmer for 3 minutes. Pour out all but 1 tablespoon of the water.
2. Add the olive oil, scallions, garlic, chili powder, and cumin to the skillet, and cook, stirring, for 2 minutes. Add the mushrooms and cook, occasionally stirring, for 5 to 7 minutes, or until the potatoes are tender and mushrooms are browned.
3. Add the tofu and 2 tablespoons of cooking water and cook until the tofu is heated through about 3 more minutes.
4. Divide the scramble among four plates and serve with tomato slices (if using).

Nutrition:

- Calories: 186
- Total Fat: 10 g
- Saturated Fat: 2 g
- Cholesterol: 0 mg
- Sodium: 33 mg
- Potassium: 672 mg
- Magnesium: 104 mg
- Total Carbs: 14 g
- Fiber: 4 g
- Sugars: 3 g
- Protein: 15 g

19. Spicy Bean Chili

Preparation Time: 15 minutes **Serving:** 4

Cooking Time: 20 minutes

Ingredients:

- 2 tsp. olive oil

- 1 medium red onion, thinly sliced
- 2 garlic cloves, minced
- 2 (15-ounce) cans kidney beans, drained and rinsed
- 1 (8-ounce) can no-salt crushed tomatoes
- 1 cup low-sodium vegetable broth
- ½ cup water
- 2 tsp. chili powder
- ¼ tsp. ground cinnamon

Description:

1. Heat the olive oil in a large saucepan over medium-high heat. Add the onion and sauté until the onion is lightly caramelized about 5 minutes. Add the garlic and sauté until fragrant, about 30 seconds.
2. Stir in the remaining ingredients and bring to a boil on high for 1 minute. Cover, reduce heat to low and simmer until flavors are well combined about 10 minutes.
3. Enjoy immediately.

Nutrition:

- Calories: 223
- Total Fat: 4g
- Saturated Fat: 0g
- Cholesterol: 0 mg
- Sodium: 237 mg
- Potassium: 170 mg
- Magnesium: 57mg
- Total Carbs: 37 g
- Fiber: 13 g
- Sugars: 1 g
- Protein: 12 g

20. Mexican Beans and Rice

Preparation Time: 5 minutes

Cooking Time: 35 minutes

Serving: 4

Ingredients:

- 1 cup uncooked medium grain brown rice
- 2 cups cold water
- 1 (14.5 ounces) can no-salt diced tomatoes in juice
- 2 tbsp. olive oil
- 6 garlic cloves, finely chopped
- 1 medium jalapeño pepper, cored, seeded, and finely chopped
- 1 (15-ounce) can black beans, drained and rinsed
- 2 tsp. cumin
- 1 tsp. chili powder
- ¼ cup finely chopped fresh oregano
- ¼ cup finely chopped fresh cilantro

Directions:

1. In a 1-quart saucepan, combine the rice with the cold water. Bring to a boil over medium-high heat. Cover, reduce heat to low, and simmer for 20 minutes.
2. Remove the pan from the heat and let stand, covered, another 5 minutes.
3. While the rice steams, set a fine colander or sieve in a bowl and drain the can of tomatoes. Pour the tomato juices into a 1-cup liquid measure. Add enough water to the tomato juice to equal 1 cup. Set the tomatoes aside.
4. Heat the olive oil in a medium skillet over medium-high heat. Add the garlic and jalapeño, and stir-fry until the garlic browns and the jalapeño smells pungent about 1 minute.
5. Add the black beans, cumin, and chili powder; stir two to three times to incorporate the mixture and cook the spices, about 30 seconds.
6. Stir in the tomato liquid and bring to a boil. Adjust the heat to maintain a gentle boil and cook, occasionally stirring, for 5 to 7 minutes, or until the beans absorb much of the liquid.
7. Add the tomatoes, oregano, cilantro, and cooked rice. Continue cooking, occasionally stirring, for 1 to 2 minutes, or until the rice is warm.

8. Serve immediately.

Nutrition:

- Calories: 356
- Total Fat: 10 g
- Saturated Fat: 1 g
- Cholesterol: 0 mg
- Sodium: 128 mg
- Potassium: 439 mg
- Magnesium: 53 mg
- Total Carbs: 59 g
- Fiber: 11 g
- Sugars: 0 g
- Protein: 11 g

Chapter 4
Side Dishes

21. Tomatoes Side Salad

Preparation time: 10 minutes

Cooking time: 0 minutes

Servings: 4

Ingredients:

- ½ bunch mint, chopped
- 8 plum tomatoes, sliced
- 1 tsp. mustard
- 1 tbsp. rosemary vinegar
- A black pepper pinch

Directions:

1. In a bowl, mix vinegar with mustard and pepper and whisk.
2. In another bowl, combine the tomatoes with the mint and the vinaigrette. Toss, arrange the plates and serve.
3. Enjoy!

Nutrition:

- Calories: 70
- Fat: 2 g
- Fiber: 2 g
- Carbs: 6 g
- Protein: 4 g

22. Squash Salsa

Preparation time: 10 minutes

Cooking time: 13 minutes

Servings: 6

Ingredients:

- 3 tbsp. olive oil
- 5 medium squash, peeled and sliced
- 1 cup pepitas, toasted
- 7 tomatillos
- A black pepper pinch
- 1 small onion, chopped
- 2 tbsp. fresh lime juice
- 2 tbsp. cilantro, chopped

Directions:

1. Heat up a pan over medium heat, add tomatillos, onion, and black pepper, stir, cook for 3 minutes, transfer to your food processor, and pulse.
2. Add lime juice and cilantro, pulse again, and transfer to a bowl.
3. Heat up your kitchen grill over high heat, drizzle the oil over squash slices. Grill them for 10 minutes; divide them according to the plates. Add pepitas and tomatillos mix on top and serve as a side dish.
4. Enjoy!

Nutrition:

- Calories: 120
- Fat: 2 g
- Fiber: 1 g
- Carbs: 7 g
- Protein: 1 g

23. . Apples and Fennel Mix

Preparation time: 10 minutes

Cooking time: 0 minutes

Ingredients:

- 3 big apples, cored and sliced
- 1 and ½ cup fennel, shredded
- 1/3 cup coconut cream

Servings: 3

- 3 tbsp. apple vinegar
- ½ tsp. caraway seeds
- Black pepper to the taste

Directions:

1. In a bowl, mix fennel with apples and toss.
2. In another bowl, mix coconut cream with vinegar, black pepper, and caraway seeds, whisk well, add over the fennel mix, toss, divide between plates and serve as a side dish.
3. Enjoy!

Nutrition:

- Calories: 130
- Fat: 3 g
- Fiber: 6 g
- Carbs: 10 g
- Protein: 3 g

24. Simple Roasted Celery Mix

Preparation time: 10 minutes

Cooking time: 25 minutes

Servings: 3

Ingredients:

- 3 celery roots, cubed
- 2 tbsp. olive oil
- A black pepper pinch
- 2 cups natural and unsweetened apple juice
- ¼ cup parsley, chopped
- ¼ cup walnuts, chopped

Directions:

1. In a baking dish, combine the celery with the oil, pepper, parsley, walnuts, and apple juice, toss to coat, introduce in the oven at 450°F, bake for 25 minutes, divide according to the plates and serve as a side dish.
2. Enjoy!

Nutrition:

- Calories: 140
- Fat: 2 g
- Fiber: 2 g
- Carbs: 7 g
- Protein: 7 g

25. Thyme Spring Onions

Preparation time: 10 minutes

Cooking time: 40 minutes

Ingredients:

- 15 spring onions
- A black pepper pinch

Servings: 8

- 1 tsp. thyme, chopped
- 1 tbsp. olive oil

Directions:

1. Put onions in a baking dish, add thyme, black pepper, and oil, toss, bake in the oven at 350°F for 40 minutes, divide between plates and serve as a side dish.
2. Enjoy!

Nutrition:

- Calories: 120
- Fat: 2 g
- Fiber: 2 g
- Carbs: 7 g
- Protein: 2 g

26. Carrot Slaw

Preparation time: 10 minutes

Cooking time: 10 minutes

Servings: 4

Ingredients:

- ¼ yellow onion, chopped
- 5 carrots, cut into thin matchsticks
- 1 tbsp. olive oil
- 1 garlic clove, minced
- 1 tbsp. Dijon mustard
- 1 tbsp. red vinegar
- A black pepper pinch
- 1 tbsp. lemon juice

Directions:

1. In a bowl, mix vinegar with black pepper, mustard, lemon juice, and whisk.
2. Heat oil to the pot over medium heat, add onions, stir and cook for 5 minutes.
3. Add garlic and carrots, stir, cook for 5 minutes more, transfer to a salad bowl, cool down, add the vinaigrette, toss, divide between plates and serve as a side dish.
4. Enjoy!

Nutrition:

- Calories: 120
- Fat: 3 g
- Fiber: 3 g
- Carbs: 7 g
- Protein: 5 g

27. Watermelon Tomato Salsa

Preparation time: 10 minutes

Cooking time: 0 minutes

Servings: 16

Ingredients:

- 4 yellow tomatoes, seedless and chopped
- A black pepper pinch
- 1 cup watermelon, seedless and chopped
- 1/3 cup red onion, chopped
- 2 jalapeno peppers, chopped
- ¼ cup cilantro, chopped
- 3 tbsp. lime juice

Directions:

1. In a bowl, mix tomatoes with watermelon, onion, and jalapeno.
2. Add cilantro, lime juice, and pepper, toss, divide between plates and serve as a side dish.
3. Enjoy!

Nutrition:

- Calories: 87
- Fat: 1 g
- Fiber: 2 g
- Carbs: 4 g
- Protein: 7 g

28. Sprouts Side Salad

Preparation time: 10 minutes

Cooking time: 0 minutes

Servings: 4

Ingredients:

- 2 zucchinis, cut with a spiralizer
- 2 cups bean sprouts
- 4 green onions, chopped
- 1 red bell pepper, chopped
-
- 1 Lime juice
- 1 tbsp. olive oil
- ½ cup cilantro, chopped
- ¾ cup almonds, chopped
- Black pepper to the taste

Directions:

1. In a salad bowl, mix zucchinis with bean sprouts, onions, and bell pepper.
2. Add black pepper, lime juice, almonds, cilantro, and olive oil, toss everything, divide between plates and serve as a side dish.
3. Enjoy!

Nutrition:

- Calories: 120
- Fat: 4 g
- Fiber: 2 g
- Carbs: 7 g
- Protein: 12 g

29. Zucchini and Brussels Sprouts Salad

Preparation time: 10 minutes

Servings: 4

Cooking time: 3 hours

Ingredients:

- 1-pound zucchinis, roughly cubed
- ½ pound Brussels sprouts, trimmed and halved
- ¼ cup veggie stock, low-sodium
- 1 tsp. cumin, ground
- 1 tsp. chili powder
- 2 tsp. avocado oil

Directions:

1. In a slow cooker, mix the sprouts with zucchini and other ingredients. Cover, and simmer for 3 hours on Low.
2. Divide between plates and serve as a side dish.

Nutrition:

- Calories: 51
- Fat: 0.9 g
- Cholesterol: 0 mg
- Sodium: 42 mg
- Carbs: 9.8 g
- Fiber: 3.8 g
- Sugars: 3.3 g
- Protein: 3.5 g
- Potassium: 547 mg

30. Cabbage Slaw

Preparation time: 10 minutes

Cooking time: 0 minutes

Servings: 4

Ingredients:

- 1 green cabbage head, shredded
- 1/3 cup coconut, shredded
- ¼ cup olive oil
- 2 tbsp. lemon juice
- ¼ cup coconut aminos
- 3 tbsp. sesame seeds
- ½ tsp. curry powder

- 1/3 tsp. turmeric powder
- ½ tsp. cumin, ground

Directions:

1. In a bowl, mix cabbage with coconut and lemon juice and stir.
2. Add oil, aminos, sesame seeds, curry powder, turmeric, and cumin. Toss to coat, and serve as a side dish.
3. Enjoy!

Nutrition:

- Calories: 130
- Fat: 4 g
- Fiber: 5 g
- Carbs: 8 g
- Protein: 6 g

Chapter 5
Vegetarian Dishes

31. Southwestern Bean-And-Pepper Salad

Preparation Time: 6 minutes

Cooking Time: 0 minutes

Serving: 4

- 1 (15-ounce) can pinto beans, drained and rinsed
- 2 bell peppers, cored and chopped
- 1 cup corn kernels (cut from 1 to 2 ears or frozen and thawed)
- Salt
- Freshly ground black pepper
- 2 limes juice
- 1 tbsp. olive oil
- 1 avocado, chopped

Ingredients:

-

Directions:

1. In a large bowl, combine beans, peppers, corn, salt, and pepper. Squeeze fresh lime juice to taste and stir in olive oil. Let the mixture stand in the refrigerator for 30 minutes.
2. Add avocado just before serving.
3. Budget-saver tip avocado prices can vary dramatically depending on their availability. In addition, while avocado in your salad can really add flavor and satiety, for an equally delicious salad, you could add a cup of cooked and chopped sweet potatoes with 1 to 2 tablespoons of sunflower seeds.

Nutrition:

- Total Calories: 245
- Total Fat: 11 g
- Saturated Fat: 2 g
- Cholesterol: 0 mg
- Sodium: 97 mg
- Potassium: 380 mg
- Total Carbs: 32 g
- Fiber: 10 g
- Sugars: 4 g
- Protein: 8 g

32. Cauliflower Mashed "Potatoes"

Preparation Time: 10 minutes

Cooking Time: 10 minutes

Serving: 4

Ingredients:

- 16 cups water (enough to cover cauliflower)
- 1 head cauliflower (about 3 pounds), trimmed and cut into florets
- 4 garlic cloves
- 1 tbsp. olive oil
- 1/4 tsp. salt
- 1/8 tsp. freshly ground black pepper
- 2 tsp. dried parsley

Directions:

1. Boil water. Add the cauliflower and garlic. Cook for about 10 minutes or until the cauliflower is fork-tender. Drain, return it back to the hot pan, and let it stand for 2 to 3 minutes with the lid on.

2. Transfer the cauliflower and garlic to a food processor or blender. Add the olive oil, salt, pepper, and purée until smooth.
3. Taste and adjust the salt and pepper. Remove to a serving bowl, add the parsley, and mix until combined.
4. Garnish with additional olive oil, if desired. Serve immediately.
5. Ingredient tip if you don't have a food processor or blender, you can make this dish just as you would traditional mashed potatoes by using a potato masher or hand blender.

Nutrition:

- Total Calories: 87
- Total Fat: 4 g
- Saturated Fat: 1 g
- Cholesterol: 0 mg
- Sodium: 210 mg
- Potassium: 654 mg
- Total Carbs: 12 g
- Fiber: 5 g
- Sugars: 0 g
- Protein: 4 g

33. Roasted Brussels Sprouts

Preparation Time: 5 minutes

Cooking Time: 20 minutes

Serving: 4

Ingredients:

- 1½ pounds Brussels sprouts, trimmed and halved
- 2 tbsp. olive oil
- ¼ tsp. salt
- ½ tsp. freshly ground black pepper

Directions:

1. Preheat the oven to 400°f.
2. Combine the Brussels sprouts and olive oil in a large mixing bowl and toss until they are evenly coated.
3. Turn the Brussels sprouts out onto a large baking sheet and flip them over, so they are cut-side down with the flat part touching the baking sheet. Sprinkle with salt and pepper.
4. Bake for 20 to 30 minutes or until the Brussels sprouts are lightly charred and crisp on the outside and toasted on the bottom. The outer leaves will be extra dark, too.
5. Serve immediately.
6. Ingredient tip when choosing Brussels sprouts, look for bright-green heads that are firm and heavy for their size. The leaves should be tightly packed. Avoid sprouts with yellowing leaves—a sign of age—or black spots—which means they could have fungus.

Nutrition:

- Total Calories. 134
- Total Fat: 8 g
- Saturated Fat: 1 g
- Cholesterol: 0 mg
- Sodium: 189 mg
- Potassium: 665 mg
- Total Carbs: 15 g
- Fiber: 7 g
- Sugars: 4 g
- Protein: 6 g

34. Broccoli with Garlic and Lemon

Preparation Time: 2 minutes

Cooking Time: 4 minutes

Ingredients:

- 1 cup water

Serving: 4

- 4 cups broccoli florets
- 1 tsp. olive oil

- 1 tbsp. minced garlic
- 1 tsp. lemon zest
- Salt
- Freshly ground black pepper

Directions:

1. In a small saucepan, bring 1 cup of water to a boil. Add the broccoli to the boiling water and cook for 2 to 3 minutes or until tender, being careful not to overcook. The broccoli should retain its bright-green color. Drain the water from the broccoli.
2. In a small sauté pan over medium-high heat, add the olive oil. Add the garlic and sauté for 30 seconds. Add the broccoli, lemon zest, salt, and pepper. Combine well and serve.
3. Ingredient tip to retain the most nutrients in your vegetables, it is important not to overcook them, as the vitamins and minerals will leach out into the cooking water. Steamer baskets are inexpensive and are a good way to cook veggies quickly. Another direction to minimize nutrient loss is to steam in the microwave by adding the vegetables to a microwave-safe dish with a couple of tbsp. of water and cooking on high for 2 to 3 minutes.

Nutrition:

- Total Calories: 38
- Total Fat: 1 g
- Saturated Fat: 0 g
- Cholesterol: 0 mg
- Sodium: 24 mg
- Potassium: 295 mg
- Total Carbs: 5 g
- Fiber: 3 g
- Sugars: 0 g
- Protein: 3g

35. Brown-Rice Pilaf

Preparation Time: 5 minutes

Serving: 4

Cooking Time: 10 minutes

Ingredients:

- 1 cup low-sodium vegetable broth
- ½ tbsp. olive oil
- 1 clove garlic, minced
- 1 scallion, thinly sliced
- 1 tbsp. minced onion flakes
- 1 cup instant brown rice
- 1/8 tsp. freshly ground black pepper

Directions:

1. Mix the vegetable broth, olive oil, garlic, scallion, and minced onion flakes in a saucepan and bring to a boil.
2. Add rice, return mixture to boil, then reduce heat and simmer for 10 minutes.
3. Remove from heat and let stand for 5 minutes.
4. Fluff with a fork and season with black pepper.

Ingredient tip: The nutritional differences between a serving of long-grain brown rice, which requires 35 to 45 minutes to cook, and instant brown rice, which cooks in about 10 minutes, is insignificant. Instant rice has simply been cooked and dehydrated, so it cooks quicker than long-grain rice. Feel free to use both varieties interchangeably.

Nutrition:

- Calories: 100
- Total Fat: 2 g
- Saturated Fat: 0 g
- Cholesterol: 0 mg
- Sodium: 35 mg
- Potassium: 24 mg
- Total Carbs: 19 g
- Fiber: 2 g
- Sugars: 1 g
- Protein: 2 g

36. Chunky Black-Bean Dip

Preparation Time: 5 minutes

Cooking Time: 1 minute

Serving: 2

Ingredients:

- 1 (15-ounce) can black beans, drained, with liquid reserved
- ½ (7-ounce) can chipotle peppers in adobo sauce
- ¼ cup plain Greek yogurt
- Freshly ground black pepper

Directions:

1. Combine beans, peppers, and yogurt in a food processor or blender and process until smooth. Add some of the bean liquid, 1 tablespoon at a time, for a thinner consistency.
2. Season to taste with black pepper.
3. Serve.

Ingredient tip: Chipotles are small peppers dried by a smoking process that gives them a dark color and a distinct smoky flavor. You can find this canned ingredient in the Latin aisle of grocery stores and big-box chains. As an alternative, you could use 1 teaspoon dry chipotle chili powder.

Nutrition:

- Total Calories: 70
- Total Fat: 1 g
- Saturated Fat: 0 g
- Cholesterol: 0 mg
- Sodium: 159 mg
- Potassium: 21 mg
- Total Carbs: 11 g
- Fiber: 4 g
- Sugars: 0 g
- Protein: 5 g

37. Classic Hummus

Preparation Time: 5 minutes

Cooking Time: 0 minutes

Serving: 6-8

Ingredients:

- 1 (15-ounce) can chickpeas, drained and rinsed
- 3 tbsp. sesame tahini
- 2 tbsp. olive oil
- 3 garlic cloves, chopped
- 1 lemon juice
- Salt
- Freshly ground black pepper

Directions:

1. In a food processor or blender, combine all the ingredients: until smooth but thick. Add water, if necessary, to produce smoother hummus.
2. Store covered for up 5 days.

Ingredient tip: Supermarkets offer a variety of different flavors of hummus, which you can easily recreate at home. For red pepper hummus, simply add 1 chopped red pepper to the ingredients. Try beets, cucumber, olives, or avocado. The possibilities are endless.

Nutrition:

- Total Calories: 147
- Total Fat: 10 g
- Saturated Fat: 1 g
- Cholesterol: 0 mg
- Sodium: 64 mg
- Potassium: 16 mg
- Total Carbs: 11 g
- Fiber: 4 g
- Sugars: 0 g
- Protein: 6 g

38. Crispy Potato Skins

Preparation Time: 2 minutes

Cooking Time: 19 minutes

Serving: 2

Ingredients:

- 2 russet potatoes
- Cooking spray
- 1 tsp. dried rosemary
- 1/8 tsp. freshly ground black pepper

Directions:

1. Preheat the oven to 375°f.
2. Wash the potatoes and pierce them several times with a fork. Place on a plate. Cook on full power in the microwave for 5 minutes. Turn over, and continue to cook for 3 to 4 minutes more, or until soft.
3. Carefully—the potatoes will be boiling—cut the potatoes in half and scoop out the pulp, leaving about 1/8 inch of potato flesh attached to the skin. Save the pulp for another use.
4. Spray the inside of each potato with cooking spray. Press in the rosemary and pepper. Place the skins on a baking sheet and bake in preheated oven for 5 to 10 minutes until slightly browned and crispy.
5. Serve immediately.

Ingredient tip: You can use any type of potato in this recipe: Yukon gold, red, or sweet, whatever fits your budget. You could also boost the calcium in this recipe by sprinkling shredded cheese on the skins before baking.

Nutrition:

- Total Calories: 114
- Total Fat: 0 g
- Saturated Fat: 0 g
- Cholesterol: 0 mg
- Sodium: 0 mg
- Potassium: 635 mg
- Total Carbs: 27 g
- Fiber: 2 g
- Sugars: 1 g
- Protein: 3 g

39. Roasted Chickpeas

Preparation Time: 5 minutes

Serving: 2

Cooking Time: 30 minutes

Ingredients:

- 1 (15-ounce can) chickpeas, drained and rinsed
- ½ tsp. olive oil
- 2 tsp. your favorite herbs or spice blend
- ¼ tsp. salt

Directions:

1. Preheat the oven to 400°f.
2. In a colander, drain and rinse the chickpeas with cold water. Cover a rimmed baking sheet with paper towels. Place the chickpeas on it in an even layer, and blot with more paper towels until most of the liquid is absorbed.
3. In a medium bowl, gently toss the chickpeas and olive oil until combined. Sprinkle the mixture with the herbs and salt and toss again.
4. Place the chickpeas back on the baking sheet and spread them in an even layer.
5. Bake for 30 to 40 minutes, until crunchy and golden brown. Stir halfway through.
6. Serve.

Ingredient tip: If you like everything bagels, try mixing together 1 teaspoon each: sesame seeds, poppy seeds, dried minced onion, and dried minced garlic—use this mixture as the seasoning in this recipe to make everything roasted chickpeas.

Nutrition:

- Total Calories: 175
- Total Fat: 3g
- Saturated Fat: 0 g
- Cholesterol: 0 mg
- Sodium: 474 mg
- Potassium: 0 mg
- Total Carbs: 29 g
- Fiber: 11 g
- Sugars: 0 g
- Protein: 11 g

40. Carrot-Cake Smoothie

Preparation Time: 5 minutes

Cooking Time: 0 minutes

Serving: 2

Ingredients:

- 1 frozen banana, peeled and diced
- 1 cup carrots, diced (peeled if preferred)
- 1 cup nonfat or low-fat milk
- ½ cup nonfat or low-fat vanilla Greek yogurt
- ½ cup ice
- ¼ cup diced pineapple, frozen
- ½ tsp. ground cinnamon
- Pinch nutmeg
- Optional toppings: chopped walnuts, grated carrots

Directions:

1. Add all of the ingredients to a blender and process until smooth and creamy.
2. Serve immediately with optional toppings as desired.

Ingredient tip: You could also use plain Greek yogurt or plain regular yogurt and add your own sweetener to this recipe. Good choices are 1 to 2 teaspoons of pure maple syrup or honey. You could also opt for a no-calorie sweetener like stevia.

Nutrition:

- Total Calories: 180 g
- Total Fat: 1 g
- Saturated Fat: 0 g
- Cholesterol: 5 mg
- Sodium: 114 mg
- Potassium: 682 mg
- Carbs: 36 g
- Fiber: 4 g
- Sugars: 25 g
- Protein 10 g

Chapter 6
Desserts

41. Hearty Cashew and Almond butter

Preparation Time: 5 minutes

Cooking Time: 0 minutes

Servings: 1 and 1/2 cups

Ingredients:

- 1 cup almonds, blanched
- 1/3 cup cashew nuts
- 2 tbsp. coconut oil
- Sunflower seeds as needed
- 1/2 tsp. cinnamon

Directions:

1. Preheat your oven to 350°F.
2. Bake almonds and cashews for 12 minutes.
3. Let them cool.
4. Transfer to a food processor and add the remaining ingredients.
5. Add oil and keep blending until smooth.
6. Serve and enjoy!

Nutrition:

- Calories: 205
- Fat: 19 g
- Protein: 2.8 g

42. The Refreshing Nutter

Preparation Time: 10 minutes

Cooking Time: 0 minute

Servings: 1

Ingredients:

- 1 tbsp. chia seeds
- 2 cups water
- 1 ounces Macadamia Nuts
- 1-2 packets Stevia, optional
- 1-ounce hazelnut

Directions:

1. Add all the listed ingredients to a blender.
2. Blend on high until smooth and creamy.
3. Enjoy your smoothie.

Nutrition:

- Calories: 452
- Fat: 43 g
- Carbs: 15 g
- Protein: 9 g

43. Elegant Cranberry Muffins

Preparation Time: 10 minutes

Cooking Time: 20 minutes

Servings: 24

Ingredients:

- 2 cups almond flour
- 2 tsp. baking soda
- 1/3 cup avocado oil
- 1 whole egg
- 3/4 cup almond milk

- 1/2 cup Erythritol
- 1/2 cup apple sauce
- 1 orange zest
- 2 tsp. ground cinnamon
- 2 cup fresh cranberries

Directions:

4. Preheat your oven to 350°F.
5. Line a muffin tin with paper muffin cups and keep them on the side.
6. Add flour, baking soda and keep it on the side.
7. Take another bowl and whisk in the remaining ingredients and add flour; mix well.
8. Pour batter into prepared muffin tin and bake for 20 minutes.
9. Once done, let it cool for 10 minutes.
10. Serve and enjoy!

Nutrition:

- Total Carbs: 7 g
- Fiber: 2 g
- Protein: 2.3 g
- Fat: 7 g

44. Cinnamon Ice Cream

Preparation Time: 10 minutes

Cooking Time: 15 minutes

Servings: 8

- 1 cinnamon stick
- 1 1/2 cup natural granulated sweetener (Stevia, Truvia, Erythritol... etc.)
- 1 1/2 tbsp. lemon peel
- 8 egg yolks from free-range chicken
- 1 pinch salt
- 1 1/2 tbsp. ground cinnamon
- 1 cup cream

Ingredients:

- 1 1/2 cup almond milk (or coconut milk)

Directions:

1. In a saucepan, heat almond milk, cinnamon stick, stevia sweetener, and lemon peel.
2. Bring to boil, reduce the heat and stir over low heat for 10 minutes,
3. In a bowl, beat the egg yolks with a pinch of salt until frothy. Place the egg mixture in a glass bowl over the double boiler and stir until thickened.
4. Remove the cinnamon stick and lemon peel, pour the almond milk in egg yolk mixture; continue until the mixture becomes thick.
5. Remove the mixture from heat, add ground cinnamon, stir; set aside and allow it to cool at room temperature.
6. In a bowl, beat the cream until double in volume.
7. Combine the cream with egg mixture and gently stir with a wooden spatula.

8. Place the ice cream in the freezer until frozen or for at least 6-8 hours.
9. Serve and enjoy!

Nutrition:

- Calories: 181
- Carbs: 6 g
- Proteins: 4 g
- Fat: 17 g
- Fiber: 2 g

45. Stylish Chocolate Parfait

Preparation Time: 2 hours **Servings:** 4

Cooking Time: 0 minute

Ingredients:

- 2 tbsp. cocoa powder
- 1 cup almond milk
- 1 tbsp. chia seeds
- Sunflower seeds inch
- 1/2 tsp. vanilla extract

Directions:

1. Take a bowl and add cocoa powder, almond milk, chia seeds, vanilla extract, and stir.
2. Transfer to dessert glass and place in your fridge for 2 hours.
3. Serve and enjoy!

Nutrition:

- Calories: 130
- Fat: 5 g
- Carbs: 7 g
- Protein: 16 g

46. Supreme Matcha Bomb

Preparation Time: 100 minutes **Servings:** 10

Cooking Time: 0 minutes

Ingredients:

- 3/4 cup hemp seeds
- 1/2 cup coconut oil
- 2 tbsp. coconut almond butter
- 1 tsp. Matcha powder
- 2 tbsp. vanilla bean extract
- 1/2 tsp. mint extract
- Liquid stevia

Directions:

1. Take your blender/food processor and add hemp seeds, coconut oil, Matcha, vanilla extract, and stevia.
2. Blend until you have a nice batter and divide into silicon molds.
3. Melt coconut almond butter and drizzle on top.
4. Let the cups chill and enjoy!

Nutrition:

- Calories: 200
- Fat: 20 g
- Carbs: 3 g
- Protein: 5 g

47. Mesmerizing Avocado and Chocolate Pudding

Servings: 2

Cooking Time: 0 minutes

Preparation Time: 30 minutes

Ingredients:

- 1 avocado, chunked
- 1 tbsp. natural sweetener such as stevia
- 2 ounces cream cheese, at room temp
- 1/4 tsp. vanilla extract
- 4 tbsp. cocoa powder, unsweetened

Directions:

1. Blend listed ingredients in a blender until smooth.
2. Divide the mix between dessert bowls, chill for 30 minutes.
3. Serve and enjoy!

Nutrition:

- Calories: 281
- Fat: 27 g
- Carbs: 12 g
- Protein: 8 g

48. Hearty Pineapple Pudding

Preparation Time: 10 minutes

Servings: 4

Cooking Time: 5 hours

Ingredients:

- 1 tsp. baking powder
- 1 cup coconut flour
- 3 tbsp. stevia
- 3 tbsp. avocado oil
- 1/2 cup coconut milk
- 1/2 cup pecans, chopped
- 1/2 cup pineapple, chopped
- 1/2 cup lemon zest, grated
- 1 cup pineapple juice, natural

Directions:

1. Grease Slow Cooker with oil.
2. Take a bowl and mix in flour, stevia, baking powder, oil, milk, pecans, pineapple, lemon zest, pineapple juice, and stir well.
3. Pour the mix into the Slow Cooker.
4. Place lid and cook on LOW for 5 hours.
5. Divide between bowls and serve.
6. Enjoy!

Nutrition:

- Calories: 188
- Fat: 3 g
- Carbs: 14 g
- Protein: 5 g

49. Healthy Berry Cobbler

Preparation Time: 10 minutes

Servings: 8

Cooking Time: 2 hours 30 minutes

Ingredients:

- 1 1/4 cups almond flour
- 1 cup coconut sugar
- 1 tsp. baking powder

- ½ tsp. cinnamon powder
- 1 whole egg
- 1/4 cup low-fat milk
- 2 tbsp. olive oil
- 2 cups raspberries
- 2 cups blueberries

Directions:

1. Take a bowl and add almond flour, coconut sugar, baking powder, and cinnamon.
2. Stir well.
3. Take another bowl and add egg, milk, oil, raspberries, blueberries, and stir.
4. Combine both of the mixtures.
5. Grease your Slow Cooker.
6. Pour the combined mixture into your Slow Cooker and cook on HIGH for 2 hours 30 minutes.
7. Divide between serving bowls and enjoy!

Nutrition:

- Calories: 250
- Fat: 4 g
- Carbs: 30 g
- Protein: 3 g

50. Tasty Poached Apples

Preparation Time: 10 minutes

Cooking Time: 2 hours 30 minutes

Servings: 8

Ingredients:

- 6 apples, cored, peeled and sliced
- 1 cup apple juice, natural
- 1 cup coconut sugar
- 1 tbsp. cinnamon powder

Directions:

1. Grease Slow Cooker with cooking spray.
2. Add apples, sugar, juice, cinnamon to your Slow Cooker.
3. Stir gently.
4. Place lid and cook on HIGH for 4 hours.
5. Serve cold and enjoy!

Nutrition:

- Calories: 180
- Fat: 5 g
- Carbs: 8 g
- Protein: 4 g

Chapter 7
Beef and Pork

51. Decent Beef and Onion Stew

Preparation Time: 10 minutes

Cooking Time: 1-2 hours

Serving: 4

- 2 pounds lean beef, cubed
- 3 pounds shallots, peeled
- 5 garlic cloves, peeled, whole
- 3 tbsp. tomato paste
- 1 bay leaves
- ¼ cup olive oil
- 3 tbsp. lemon juice

Ingredients:

Direction:

1. Take a stew pot and place it over medium heat.
2. Add olive oil and let it heat up.
3. Add meat and brown.
4. Add the remaining ingredients and cover with water.
5. Bring the whole mix to a boil.
6. Reduce heat to low and cover the pot.
7. Simmer for 1-2 hours until beef is cooked thoroughly.
8. Serve hot!

Nutrition

- Calories: 136
- Fat: 3 g
- Carbs: 0.9 g
- Protein: 24 g

52. Zucchini Beef Sauté with Coriander Greens

Preparation Time: 10 minutes

Cooking Time: 10 minutes

Serving: 4

Ingredients:

- 10 ounces beef, sliced into 1-2-inch strips
- 1 zucchini, cut into 2-inch strips
- ¼ cup parsley, chopped
- 3 garlic cloves, minced
- 2 tbsp. tamari sauce
- 4 tbsp. avocado oil

Direction:

1. Add 2 tbsp. of avocado oil in a frying pan over high heat.
2. Place strips of beef and brown for a few minutes on high heat.
3. Once the meat is brown, add zucchini strips and sauté until tender.

4. Once tender, add tamari sauce, garlic, parsley and let them sit for a few minutes more.
5. Serve immediately and enjoy!

Nutrition

- Calories: 500
- Fat: 40 g
- Carbs: 5 g
- Protein: 31 g

53. Beef Soup

Preparation Time: 10 minutes

Serving: 4

Cooking Time: 40 minutes

Ingredients:

- 1-pound ground beef, lean
- 1 cup mixed vegetables, frozen
- 1 yellow onion, chopped
- 6 cups vegetable broth
- 1 cup low-fat cream
- Pepper to taste

Direction:

1. Take a stockpot and add all the ingredients except heavy cream, salt, and black pepper.
2. Bring to a boil.
3. Reduce heat to simmer.
4. Cook for 40 minutes.
5. Once cooked, warm the heavy cream.
6. Then add once the soup is cooked.
7. Blend the soup till smooth by using an immersion blender.
8. Season with salt and black pepper.
9. Serve and enjoy!

Nutrition

- Calories: 270
- Fat: 14 g
- Carbs: 6 g
- Protein: 29 g

54. Almond Butter Pork Chops

Preparation Time: 5 minutes

Serving: 2

Cooking Time: 25 minutes

Ingredients:

- 1 tbsp. almond butter, divided
- 2 boneless pork chops
- Pepper to taste
- 1 tbsp. dried Italian seasoning, low fat and low sodium
- 1 tbsp. olive oil

Directions:

1. Preheat your oven to 350°F.
2. Pat pork chops dry with a paper towel and place them in a baking dish.
3. Season with pepper and Italian seasoning.
4. Drizzle olive oil over pork chops.
5. Top each chop with ½ tablespoon of almond butter.
6. Bake for 25 minutes.
7. Transfer pork chops on two plates and top with almond butter juice.
8. Serve and enjoy!

Nutrition:

- Calories: 333
- Fat: 23 g
- Carbs: 1 g
- Protein: 31 g

55. Hearty Pork Belly Casserole

Preparation Time: 5 minutes

Cooking Time: 25 minutes

Serving: 4

Ingredients:

- 8 pork belly slices, cut into small pieces
- 3 large onions, chopped
- 4 tbsp. lemon
- 1 lemon juice
- Seasoning as you needed

Direction:

1. Take a large pressure cooker and place it over medium heat.
2. Add onions and sweat them for 5 minutes.
3. Add pork belly slices and cook until the meat browns and onions become golden.
4. Cover with water and add honey, lemon zest, sunflower seeds, pepper, and close the pressure seal.
5. Pressure cook for 40 minutes.
6. Serve and enjoy with a garnish of fresh chopped parsley if you prefer.

Nutrition

- Calories: 753
- Fat: 41 g
- Carbs: 68 g
- Protein: 30 g

56. Healthy Avocado Beef Patties

Preparation Time: 15 minutes

Cooking Time: 10 minutes

Serving: 2

Ingredients:

- 1 pound 85% lean ground beef
- 1 small avocado, pitted and peeled
- Fresh ground black pepper as needed

Directions:

1. Preheat and prepare your broiler to high.
2. Divide beef into two equal-sized patties.
3. Season the patties with pepper accordingly.
4. Broil the patties for 5 minutes per side.
5. Transfer the patties to a platter.
6. Slice avocado into strips and place them on top of the patties.
7. Serve and enjoy!

Nutrition

- Calories: 568
- Fat: 43 g
- Net Carbs: 9 g
- Protein: 38 g

57. Ravaging Beef Pot Roast

Preparation Time: 10 minutes

Cooking Time: 75 minutes

Serving: 4

Ingredients:

- 3 ½ pounds beef roast
- 4 ounces mushrooms, sliced
- 12 ounces beef stock
- 1-ounce onion soup mix
- ½ cup Italian dressing, low sodium, and low fat

Directions:

1. Take a bowl and add the stock, onion soup mix, and Italian dressing.

2. Stir.
3. Put beef roast in the pan.
4. Add mushrooms, stock mix to the pan, and cover with foil.
5. Preheat your oven to 300°F.
6. Bake for 1 hour and 15 minutes.
7. Let the roast cool.
8. Slice and serve.
9. Enjoy with the gravy on top!

Nutrition

- Calories: 700
- Fat: 56 g
- Carbs: 10 g
- Protein: 70 g

58. Crazy Japanese Potato and Beef Croquettes

Preparation Time: 10 minutes

Serving: 10

Cooking Time: 20 minutes

Ingredients:

- 3 medium russet potatoes, peeled and chopped
- 1 tbsp. almond butter
- 1 tbsp. vegetable oil
- 3 onions, diced
- ¾ pound ground beef
- 4 tsp. light coconut aminos
- All-purpose flour for coating
- 2 eggs, beaten
- Panko bread crumbs for coating
- ½ cup oil, frying

Directions:

1. Take a saucepan, place it over medium-high heat; add potatoes and sunflower seeds water. Boil for 16 minutes.
2. Remove water and put potatoes in another bowl. Add almond butter and mash the potatoes.
3. Take a frying pan and place it over medium heat. Add 1 tablespoon of oil and let it heat up.
4. Add onions and stir fry until tender.
5. Add coconut aminos to beef to onions.
6. Keep frying until beef is browned.
7. Mix the beef with the potatoes evenly.
8. Take another frying pan and place it over medium heat; add half a cup of oil.
9. Form croquettes using the mashed potato mixture and coat them with flour, then eggs, and finally breadcrumbs.
10. Fry patties until golden on all sides.
11. Enjoy!

Nutrition

- Calories: 239
- Fat: 4 g
- Carbs: 20 g
- Protein: 10 g

59. Cool Cabbage Fried Beef

Preparation Time: 5 minutes

Serving: 4

Cooking Time: 15 minutes

Ingredients:

- 1-pound beef, ground and lean
- ½ pound bacon
- 1 onion
- 1 garlic clove, minced
- ½ head cabbage
- Pepper to taste

Directions:

1. Take a skillet and place it over medium heat.
2. Add chopped bacon, beef, and onion until slightly browned.
3. Transfer to a bowl and keep it covered.
4. Add minced garlic and cabbage to the skillet and cook until slightly browned.
5. Return the ground beef mixture to the skillet and simmer for 3-5 minutes over low heat.
6. Serve and enjoy!

Nutrition

- Calories: 360
- Fat: 22 g
- Net Carbs: 5 g
- Protein: 34 g

60. Pork, White Bean, and Spinach Soup

Preparation Time: 10 minutes
Serving: 4
Cooking Time: 15 minutes

Ingredients:

- 1 tbsp. olive oil
- 8 ounces pork tenderloin or boneless pork chops, cut into 1-inch cubes
- Salt
- 4 garlic cloves, minced
- 2 tsp. paprika
- 1 (14.5-ounce) can diced salt-free tomatoes
- 4 cups low-sodium chicken broth
- 1 bunch spinach, ribs removed and chopped, about 8 cups, lightly packed
- 2 (15-ounce) cans white beans, drained and rinsed

Directions:

1. Heat the oil in a Dutch oven or heavy-bottom pot over medium-high heat. Season pork with a pinch of salt. When the pan is hot, add pork and cook, occasionally stirring, for about 2 minutes, or long enough to encourage a good sear and brown sides. Transfer to a plate.
2. In the same pot, add garlic and paprika. Cook, stirring often, until fragrant (about 30 seconds). Add tomatoes and increase heat to high, and stir to scrape down any browned bits. Add broth and bring to a boil.
3. Add spinach until it just wilts (about 2 to 3 minutes). Reduce heat to maintain a simmer, stir in the beans, reserved pork, and any accumulated juices; simmer until the beans and pork are heated through (about 2 minutes).
4. Serve immediately.

Nutrition:

- Total Calories: 327
- Total Fat: 8 g
- Saturated Fat: 2 g
- Cholesterol: 22 mg
- Sodium: 389 mg
- Potassium: 511 mg
- Total Carbs: 41 g
- Fiber: 15 g
- Sugars: 5 g
- Protein: 26 g

Chapter 8
Soups

61. Curried Kabocha Squash Soup

Preparation Time: 10 minutes

Cooking Time: 10 minutes

Servings: 4

- 4 cups water
- ¼ cups oats
- 4-6 garlic cloves
- 1 tbsp. seasoning
- 2 tsp. smoked paprika
- 1 tsp. curry powder
- ¼ tsp. ground ginger
- ¼ tsp. ground turmeric
- 4 cups almond milk

Ingredients:

- 8 cups cooked Kabocha squash

Directions:

1. Carefully cook your squash first before following the remaining recipe if you have not cooked already.
2. Cut the cooked squash in half and deseed them.
3. Add the squash alongside the listed ingredients (except milk) to your Instant Pot.
4. Lock up the lid and cook on HIGH pressure for 5 minutes.
5. Perform a natural release over 10 minutes.
6. Add almond milk.
7. Take an immersion blender and puree the soup.
8. Set your pot to Sauté mode and allow the soup to thicken.
9. Serve!

Nutrition:

- Calories: 106
- Fat: 0 g
- Carbs: 28 g
- Protein: 2 g

62. Kale and Potato Soup Straight From Ireland

Preparation Time: 10 minutes

Cooking Time: 20 minutes

Servings: 6

- 2 tbsp. olive oil
- 2 cups leek
- 6 cups vegetable broth
- 2-pound potatoes
- 2 cloves minced garlic
- 8-ounce kale
- ½ a tsp. apple cider vinegar
- Freshly ground black pepper
- Chopped green onion

Ingredients:

Directions:

1. Set your pot to Sauté mode and add oil, allow the oil to heat up.
2. Add leeks and Sauté for 8-10 minutes.
3. Add vegetable broth, garlic, and potatoes and lock up the lid.
4. Cook on HIGH pressure for 6 minutes.
5. Quick-release the pressure mashes the potatoes.
6. Stir in chopped-up kale and lock up the lid again.
7. Cook on HIGH pressure for 2 minutes.
8. Stir in apple cider vinegar, season with flavored vinegar, and a grind of black pepper.
9. Serve with a garnish of green onion.
10. Enjoy!

Nutrition:

- Calories: 230
- Carbs: 54 g
- Protein: 10 g

63. Potato and Carrot "Impeccable" Soup

Preparation Time: 15 minutes

Cooking Time: 10 minutes

Servings: 2

Ingredients:

- 5 medium-sized chopped and peeled potatoes
- 8 peeled and chopped carrots
- ½ a chopped yellow onion
- 3 minced garlic cloves
- 2 cups finely chopped fresh kale
- 1 tbsp. curry powder
- 1 tsp. cayenne pepper
- 4 cups water
- 2 cups vegetable broth

Directions:

1. Mince up garlic and chop up the onions.
2. Add ¼ cup of water to the pot and set the pot to Sauté mode.
3. Add onions and garlic and Sauté for 5 minutes.
4. Add vegetable broth, cayenne, powdered peanut butter, and curry powder.
5. Stir everything well. Add water and Sauté for 2 minutes.
6. Add the remaining ingredients (except kale) and seal the lid.
7. Cook on HIGH pressure for 8 minutes. Release the pressure naturally.
8. Open the lid and take an immersion blender to puree the soup.
9. Add chopped-up kale and mix well. Serve and enjoy!

Nutrition:

- Calories: 128
- Fat: 4 g
- Carbs: 20 g
- Protein: 3 g

64. Meticulous Butternut Squash Soup

Preparation Time: 5 minutes

Cooking Time: 30 minutes

Servings: 4

Ingredients:

For Soup:

- 1 tsp. extra virgin olive oil
- 1 large-sized chopped up onion
- 2 minced garlic cloves
- 1 tbsp. curry powder
- 3 pounds butternut squash, cut up into 1-inch cubes and peeled
- 3 cups water
- ½ a cup coconut milk

For Extra Toppings:

- Hulled up pumpkin seeds
- Dried up cranberries

Directions:

1. Set the pot to Sauté mode and add olive oil, allow the oil to heat up
2. Add onions and Sauté for 8 minutes
3. Add garlic and curry powder and Sauté for 1 minute
4. Cancel the Sauté mode and add butternut squash, water, and flavored vinegar
5. Lock up the lid and cook on HIGH pressure for 30 minutes
6. Release the pressure naturally over 10 minutes
7. Open the lid and blend using an immersion blender
8. Stir in coconut milk and season
9. Serve topped with cranberries/pumpkin seeds
10. Enjoy!

Nutrition:

- Calories: 124
- Fat: 6 g
- Carbs: 18 g
- Protein: 2 g

65. "Split" Pea and Sundried Tomatoes Soup

Preparation Time: 5 minutes

Servings: 4

Cooking Time: 8 minutes

Ingredients:

- 1 pound green split peas
- 1 chopped large onion
- 1 pound sliced carrot
- 1 sliced heart celery
- 2 large potatoes cubed up
- 2 cups chopped sundried tomatoes
- 1 small cremini mushroom dried
- 6-8 cloves garlic
- 4 tsp. dried parsley
- 1-2 tbsp. flavored vinegar
- 1 tsp. dried basil
- 1 tsp. dried rosemary
- 1 tsp. dried oregano
- 1 tsp. celery seed
- 1 tsp. smoked paprika
- 1 piece bay leaf

Directions:

1. Add the listed ingredients to your Instant Pot
2. Lock up the lid and cook on HIGH pressure for 8 minutes
3. Release the pressure naturally over 10 minutes
4. Serve it over brown rice. Enjoy!

Nutrition:

- Calories: 306
- Fat: 9 g
- Carbs: 46 g
- Protein: 16 g

66. House's Special Cashew Spring Green Soup

Preparation Time: 25 minutes

Servings: 4

Cooking Time: 20 minutes

Ingredients:

- 2 tbsp. extra virgin olive oil
- 3 pieces leeks
- 2 minced cloves garlic
- 2 seeded and veins removed Serrano chiles chopped up
- 6 and ¼ cups vegetable broth
- 2 small Yukon gold potatoes peeled up and cut into ½ inch dice
- 10 ounces spring greens salad mix
- 2 tsp. of ground turmeric
- ½ a tsp. flavored sea vinegar
- 1 and a ¼ cup raw cashew soaked
- 2 tsp. white miso

Directions:

1. Set the pot to Sauté mode and add oil, allow the oil to heat up.
2. Add leeks and Sauté for 5 minutes.
3. Stir in pepper and garlic and 5 cups of broth.
4. Add potatoes, spring greens mix, and add turmeric.
5. Season with flavored vinegar.
6. Lock up the lid and cook on HIGH pressure for 6 minutes.
7. Release the pressure naturally over 10 minutes.
8. Set your pot to Sauté mode and add soaked cashews, 1 and ¼ cup of broth and blend the mixture using an immersion blender.
9. Add miso cream and blend again.
10. Add lime juice, 10 grinds of pepper.
11. Season with a bit of more flavored vinegar.
12. Ladle the soup into bowls and decorate with a swirl of cashew cream.
13. Enjoy!

Nutrition:

- Calories: 388
- Fat: 17 g
- Carbs: 49 g
- Protein: 11 g

67. Omnipotent Organic Chicken Thigh Soup

Preparation Time: 5 minutes

Servings: 4

Cooking Time: 45 minutes

Ingredients:

- 2 pounds organic chicken thigh
- 1 cup fresh pineapple chunks
- ½ a cup coconut cream
- 1 tsp. cinnamon
- 1/8 tsp. flavored vinegar
- 2 tbsp. coconut aminos
- ½ a cup chopped up green onion

Directions:

1. Set your pot to Sauté mode and add ghee.
2. Allow the ghee to melt and add diced-up onion, cook for about 5 minutes until the onions. are caramelized. Add pressed garlic, ham, broth, and simmer for 2-3 minutes.
3. Add thyme and asparagus and lock up the lid.
4. Cook on SOUP mode for 45 minutes. Release the pressure naturally and enjoy!

Nutrition:

- Calories: 161
- Fat: 8 g
- Carbs: 16 g
- Protein: 6 g

68. Very Low Carb Ham and Cabbage Bowl

Preparation Time: 15 minutes

Servings: 6

Cooking Time: 15 minutes

Ingredients:

- 1 chopped cabbage head
- 1 finely chopped onion
- 1 finely chopped red bell pepper
- 2 small carrots cut up into rounds
- 2 cups diced lean ham
- 2 pieces bay leaves
- 1 tsp. all-purpose seasoning
- 1 tsp. granulated garlic
- 1 tbsp. dried parsley
- 1 tsp. seasoning flavored vinegar
- 6 cups chicken stock
- Parmesan cheese for serving

Directions:

1. Chop up the cabbage, red bell pepper, onion, ham, and carrots.
2. Add the onion, cabbage, and red bell pepper to the Instant Pot.
3. Add chopped ham, carrots alongside bay leaves.
4. Sprinkle seasoning flavored vinegar on top, all-purpose seasoning, dried parsley, and granulated garlic. Lock up the lid and cook on HIGH pressure for 15 minutes.
5. Release the pressure naturally over 10 minutes.
6. Serve hot with grated parmesan on top. Enjoy!

Nutrition:

- Calories: 296
- Fat: 25 g
- Carbs: 2 g
- Protein: 17 g

69. Cabbage and Leek Soup

Preparation Time: 10 minutes

Cooking Time: 25 minutes

Servings: 4

Ingredients:

- 2 tbsp. coconut oil
- ½ a head chopped up cabbage
- 3-4 diced ribs celery
- 2-3 carefully cleaned and chopped leeks
- 1 diced bell pepper
- 2-3 diced carrots
- 2/3 cloves minced garlic
- 4 cups chicken broth
- 1 tsp. Italian seasoning
- 1 tsp. Creole seasoning
- Black pepper as needed
- 2-3 cups of mixed salad greens

Directions:

1. Set your pot to Sauté mode and add coconut oil
2. Allow the oil to heat up.
3. Add the veggies (except salad greens) starting from the carrot, making sure to stir it well. after each vegetable addition.
4. Make sure to add the garlic last.
5. Season with Italian seasoning, black pepper, and Creole seasoning.
6. Add broth and lock up the lid.
7. Cook on SOUP mode for 20 minutes.
8. Release the pressure naturally and add salad greens, stir well and allow it to sit for a while.
9. Allow for a few minutes to wilt the veggies.
10. Season with a bit of flavored vinegar and pepper and enjoy!

Nutrition:

- Calories: 32
- Fat: 0 g
- Carbs: 4 g
- Protein: 2 g

70. Quinoa and Lentil Soup

Preparation Time: 10 minutes

Cooking Time: 25 minutes

Servings: 4

Ingredients:

- 1 chopped up medium onion
- 3 chopped up celery stalks and leaves
- 1 cup chopped up fennel
- 1 tbsp. chopped up garlic

- 1 and a ½ tsp. of curry powder
- 1 tsp. flavored vinegar
- 1 tbsp. freshly grated ginger
- 1 tbsp. freshly grated turmeric
- 6 cups vegetable stock
- 1 can of 14 ounces of organic coconut milk
- 1/3 cup quinoa
- ¼ cup green lentils
- 3 peeled and chopped carrots
- ½ a head cauliflower broken apart
- 1 and a 1/2 cup curly leaf kale, finely chopped up
- ¼ cup chopped cilantro
- Flavored vinegar as needed
- Pepper as needed
- Cayenne pepper as needed

Directions:

1. Add onion, fennel, celery, flavored vinegar, curry powder, quinoa, turmeric, ginger, lentils, and stock to your pot.
2. Lock up the lid and cook on HIGH pressure for 15 minutes.
3. Release the pressure naturally.
4. Open the lid and add cauliflower, carrots and set your pot to sauté mode
5. Simmer for 5-10 minutes.
6. Add cilantro and kale, season with some pepper to spice things up.

Nutrition:

- Calories: 174
- Fat: 1 g
- Carbs: 33 g
- Protein: 8 g

Chapter 9
Fish and Seafood

71. Tilapia Tacos with Chipotle Cream

Preparation Time: 5 minutes

Cooking Time: 10 minutes

Serving: 2

Ingredients:

- 1 tsp. olive oil
- 10 to 12 ounces tilapia
- 1 tsp. chili powder
- 1/2 tsp. ground cumin
- 1/8 tsp. salt
- 4 (6-inch) flour tortillas

For the Sauce:

- ½ tsp. smoked paprika
- ¼ tsp. cayenne pepper, or to taste
- ½ cup nonfat Greek yogurt
- 1 chipotle pepper in adobo sauce, chopped

Directions:

To Make Tacos:

1. Heat the oil in a medium skillet on medium-high heat. Add the tilapia to the hot skillet and sprinkle it with chili powder, cumin, and salt. Cook for 3 to 4 minutes per side. Remove the fish from the heat and gently flake it into bite-size pieces.
2. Wrap the tortillas in a paper towel and heat them for 1 minute in the microwave on high.

To Make the Sauce:

1. In a small bowl, mix together the paprika and cayenne pepper. Add the yogurt and chopped chipotle pepper to the spices, blending well.
2. Divide the fish between the tortillas, top with a spoon of the chipotle cream, and serve.

Nutrition:

- Calories: 383
- Total Fat: 9 g
- Carbs: 36 g
- Fiber: 3 g
- Protein: 40 g
- Calcium: 168 mg
- Sodium: 716 mg
- Potassium: 727 mg
- Vitamin D: 2 mcg
- Iron: 4 mg
- Zinc: 1 mg

72. Baked Haddock with Peppers & Eggplant

Preparation Time: 15 minutes

Cooking Time: 20 minutes

Serving: 2-3

Ingredients:

- Nonstick cooking spray
- 2 (5- to 6-ounce) haddock fillets
- ½ tsp. salt-free Italian seasoning
- 1 tsp. olive oil
- 2 garlic cloves, pressed or minced
- ½ cup diced onion
- 5 to 6 mini bell peppers, chopped
- 1 small eggplant, peeled and diced
- 6 large green olives, pitted and sliced
- 2 tbsp. tomato paste
- 2 tbsp. balsamic vinegar
- 1 tbsp. granulated sugar

Directions:

1. Preheat the oven to 375°F. Add cooking spray to a 9-by-11-inch baking dish with. Place the fish in the prepared baking dish, sprinkle it with the seasoning, and bake for 15 or 20 minutes, until opaque.
2. Meanwhile, in a large saucepan, heat the oil over medium heat. Add the garlic and cook for 1 minute. Add the onion and cook for 2 to 3 minutes.
3. Add the peppers and eggplant. Reduce the heat to low, cover, and allow the vegetables to steam until tender, about 6 minutes. Add a few spoons of water if needed.
4. Add the olives, tomato paste, vinegar, and sugar to the eggplant mixture and stir to combine. If needed, add a few more spoonfuls of water. Cover and simmer for 10 minutes, stirring occasionally.
5. To serve, top each serving of fish with ¾ cup of caponata.

Nutrition:

- Calories: 357
- Total Fat: 6 g
- Carbs: 51 g
- Fiber: 13 g
- Protein: 30 g
- Calcium: 107 mg
- Sodium: 425 mg
- Potassium: 1876 mg
- Vitamin D: 0 mcg
- Iron: 3 mg
- Zinc: 2 mg

73. Tex-Mex Cod with Roasted Peppers & Corn

Preparation Time: 10 minutes

Cooking Time: 30 minutes

Serving: 2

Ingredients:

- 6 mini bell peppers, assorted colors, quartered
- 1 cup frozen corn
- 2 tsp. olive oil, divided
- 1 tbsp. salt-free Tex-Mex or mesquite seasoning, divided
- Nonstick cooking spray
- 2 (6- to 8-ounce) haddock fillets
- 1 lime, quartered
- ¼ cup plain Greek yogurt, seasoned with ¼ tsp. salt-free Tex-Mex seasoning (optional)

Directions:

1. Line a baking sheet with parchment paper or a silicone mat.
2. Spread the peppers and corn evenly over two-thirds of the baking sheet. Drizzle 1 tablespoon of oil over the vegetables. Then sprinkle them with 2 tablespoons of the seasoning. Put the vegetables in the oven for 10 minutes to begin roasting. Remove the baking sheet from the oven.
3. While the vegetables roast, put cooking spray on a sheet of aluminum foil and place the fish on it. Drizzle the fish with the remaining oil and season it with the remaining 1 teaspoon of seasoning. Squeeze one lime wedge

onto each fillet. Fold up the edges of the foil, so the juices don't escape, and transfer the fish to the baking sheet with the vegetables.

4. Return the baking sheet to the oven and bake for an additional 15 to 20 minutes until the fish is opaque, white and flaky and the vegetables are tender and lightly charred.

5. Place a fish fillet on each plate, and top each with half of the roasted vegetables. Serve with a dollop of seasoned yogurt (if using).

Nutrition:

- Calories: 340
- Total Fat: 7 g
- Carbs: 38 g
- Fiber: 5 g
- Protein: 36 g
- Calcium: 84 mg
- Sodium: 382 mg
- Potassium: 1316 mg
- Vitamin D: 1 mcg
- Iron: 2 mg
- Zinc: 2 mg

74. Marinated Lime Grilled Shrimp

Preparation Time: 10 minutes

Cooking Time: 30 minutes

Serving: 2

Ingredients:

- 1 lime, quartered, divided
- ¼ cup chopped fresh cilantro, divided
- 1 tbsp. rice wine vinegar
- 1 tsp. avocado oil
- ¼ tsp. chili powder
- ¼ tsp. garlic powder
- 6 large shrimp, peeled and deveined

Directions:

1. In a small bowl, mix together the juice from three lime quarters, 3 tablespoons of cilantro, and the vinegar, oil, chili powder, and garlic powder.

2. Place the shrimp in the bowl with the marinade, toss to coat, and refrigerate it for 30 minutes or up to 4 hours.

3. Preheat a grill to medium-high. Place the shrimp on a grill pan and cook for 3 to 5 minutes, until white, turning once. Discard the marinade.

4. If you do not have a grill, pan-sear the shrimp in a nonstick skillet for 3 to 4 minutes, turning once.

5. Serve the shrimp with a squeeze of juice from the last lime quarter and the remaining cilantro.

Nutrition:

- Calories: 44
- Total Fat: 2 g
- Carbs: 3 g
- Fiber: 0 g
- Protein: 3 g
- Calcium: 18 mg
- Sodium: 131 mg
- Potassium: 74 mg
- Vitamin D: 0 mcg
- Iron: 0 mg
- Zinc: 0 mg

75. Shrimp & Broccoli with Angel Hair

Preparation Time: 10 minutes

Cooking Time: 15 minutes

Serving: 2

Ingredient:

- Salt pinch
- 4 tsp. olive oil, divided
- 1 garlic clove, pressed or minced
- 1 broccoli head, cut into florets
- 12 frozen, cooked large shrimp, peeled, deveined, and tails removed
- 4 ounces angel hair pasta
- 2 tbsp. Parmesan cheese
- Freshly ground black pepper (optional)

Directions:

1. Fill three-quarters of the large soup pot with water, add salt, and boil over high heat.
2. Heat 1 teaspoon of oil in a medium skillet over medium-high heat. Add the garlic and cook for 1 minute. Add the broccoli and sauté for 3 to 4 minutes. Cover and let the vegetable steam for an additional 2 minutes. The broccoli should be bright green and fork-tender. Set aside the heat.
3. Add the angel hair to the boiling water and cook for 2 to 4 minutes, according to the directions on the package. Drain and immediately add to the skillet. Add the remaining 1 tablespoon of olive oil and stir. Return to low heat to heat through, about 3 minutes.
4. Divide the pasta between two dishes and garnish with the Parmesan cheese and pepper to taste (if using).

Nutrition:

- Calories: 456
- Total Fat: 12 g
- Carbs: 64 g
- Fiber: 10 g
- Protein: 25 g
- Calcium: 230 mg
- Sodium: 583 mg
- Potassium: 1158 mg
- Vitamin D: 0 mcg
- Iron: 4 mg
- Zinc: 3 mg

76. Saucy Penne with Shrimp, Peas & Walnuts

Preparation Time: 5 minutes **Serving:** 2

Cooking Time: 20 minutes

Ingredients:

- 1 tsp. olive oil
- 12 large cooked frozen shrimp (peeled and deveined), thawed
- 1 cup frozen peas
- ½ cup chopped walnuts
- ½ tsp. salt-free Italian seasoning blend
- 2 tsp. unsalted butter
- 1 tbsp. all-purpose flour
- 1 cup 1 percent milk
- 2 tbsp. light cream cheese
- ¼ cup grated Parmesan cheese, divided
- 4 ounces penne pasta
- Freshly ground black pepper

Directions:

1. In a medium saucepan, heat the oil over medium-high heat and sauté the shrimp, peas, walnuts, and seasoning for 3 to 4 minutes. (Make sure any liquid from the shrimp is evaporated.) Transfer the mixture to a small bowl.
2. Wipe out the saucepan with a paper towel and melt the butter in it over medium heat. Whisk in the flour for 1 minute.
3. Slowly pour in the milk and bring it to a boil, whisking occasionally.
4. Reduce the heat to low, simmer, and stir in the cream cheese until it melts about 3 minutes.
5. Add 3 tablespoons of the Parmesan cheese and continue stirring until the sauce is creamy and well-blended about 2 minutes.
6. Add more milk if the sauce gets too thick. Remove it from the heat.

7. When the water is boiling, add the penne and boil for 8 to 9 minutes (or follow the package directions for al dente).
8. Drain the pasta and add it to the sauce. Stir to combine.
9. Transfer the pasta to a serving dish and top it with the shrimp mixture.
10. Garnish the pasta with the remaining Parmesan cheese, season it with pepper, and serve.

Nutrition:

- Calories: 673
- Total Fat: 34 g
- Carbs: 64 g
- Fiber: 6 g
- Protein: 31 g
- Calcium: 390 mg
- Sodium: 653 mg
- Potassium: 698 mg
- Vitamin D: 1 mcg
- Iron: 3 mg
- Zinc: 4 mg

77. Angel Hair with Smoked Salmon & Asparagus

Preparation Time: 15 minutes **Serving:** 2

Cooking Time: 15 minutes

Ingredients:

- 20 asparagus spears, trimmed and cut into 2-inch pieces
- 2 tbsp. olive oil, divided
- 4 ounces angel hair pasta
- 2 ounces smoked salmon, cut into bite-size pieces
- 1 tsp. capers
- 2 tbsp. grated Parmesan cheese
- Freshly ground black pepper

Directions:

1. Fill a large stockpot three-quarters full with water and bring it to a boil over high heat.
2. Add 2 tablespoons of water to a large nonstick skillet over medium heat. When the water is simmering, add the asparagus, cover, and steam for 6 minutes. Remove the lid, drain off any remaining water. Add 1½ teaspoon of oil, and sauté for 1 to 2 more minutes.
3. Add the angel hair pasta to the boiling water and cook for 3 minutes (or according to the package directions). Drain the pasta, transfer it to a serving bowl, and add the asparagus, smoked salmon, the remaining 1½ tablespoon of oil, and the capers; toss gently.
4. Serve topped with the Parmesan cheese and seasoned to taste with pepper.

Nutrition:

- Calories: 416
- Total Fat: 17 g
- Carbs: 49 g
- Fiber: 5 g
- Protein: 18 g
- Calcium: 97 mg
- Sodium: 320 mg
- Potassium: 509 mg
- Vitamin D: 5 mcg
- Iron: 6 mg
- Zinc: 2 mg

78. Bass with Citrus Butter

Preparation Time: 15 minutes **Serving:** 2

Cooking Time: 15 minutes

Ingredients:

- 2 (5- to 7-ounce) bass fillets, skin-on
- 1 tsp. salt-free seafood seasoning
- 1/8 tsp. salt
- 1 lime, halved
- 1 tbsp. avocado oil, divided

- 1 tsp. butter
- 1/4 tsp. cumin
- 1/4 cup slivered, blanched almonds

Directions:

1. Season the fish with the seasoning blend and salt.
2. In a microwave-safe glass measuring cup, stir together the juice of half a lime, 2 teaspoon of oil, butter, and cumin until blended. Set aside.
3. Heat a large nonstick skillet over medium heat. Add the almonds and toast for 2 to 3 minutes, being careful they don't over-brown. Transfer the almonds to a small bowl and set aside.
4. Heat the remaining oil in the skillet over medium-high heat. Add the bass fillets, skin side up. Sear for 3 minutes without disturbing the fillets. Then turn them and finish cooking for another 3 to 4 minutes.
5. While the fish is searing, heat the citrus butter sauce for 20 seconds in the microwave.
6. Transfer the fish to a serving dish, pour the citrus butter over it, and top it with the toasted almonds. Garnish with the remaining lime half cut into wedges and serve.

Nutrition:

- Calories: 325
- Total Fat: 21 g
- Carbs: 5 g
- Fiber: 2 g
- Protein: 30 g
- Calcium: 156 mg
- Sodium: 270 mg
- Potassium: 634 mg
- Vitamin D: 13 mcg
- Iron: 3 mg
- Zinc: 1 mg

79. Seared Mahi-Mahi with Lemon & Parsley

Preparation Time: 20 minutes

Serving: 2

Cooking Time: 15 minutes

Ingredients:

- 2 tsp. avocado oil
- 1/2 lemon juice
- 1/2 tsp. oregano
- 1/2 tsp. garlic powder
- 1/4 tsp. Worcestershire sauce
- 2 (5- to 7-ounce) mahi-mahi steaks
- 1 tbsp. chopped parsley
- 1/2 lemon, cut into two wedges

Directions:

1. Preheat the oven to 400°F. (If you'll be marinating the fish for longer than 15 minutes, preheat the oven just before baking.) Line a baking sheet with parchment paper or a silicone mat.
2. In a medium bowl, stir together the oil, lemon juice, oregano, garlic powder, and Worcestershire sauce. Put the fish in a medium zip-top plastic bag and add the marinade. Press out any excess air, seal the bag, and marinate the fish in the refrigerator for 15 minutes or up to 2 hours.
3. Remove the fish from the marinade, place it on the prepared baking sheet, and roast it for 15 minutes (discard the marinade).
4. To serve, garnish each mahi-mahi steak with parsley and a lemon wedge.

Nutrition:

- Calories: 282
- Total Fat: 18 g
- Carbs: 3 g
- Protein: 26 g
- Calcium: 41 mg
- Sodium: 101 mg
- Potassium: 594 mg
- Vitamin D: 16 mcg
- Iron: 1 mg
- Zinc: 1mg

80. Maple-Glazed Salmon

Preparation Time: 15 minutes

Serving: 2

Cooking Time: 20 minutes

Ingredients:

- 2 (5- to 6-ounce) salmon fillets, skin-on
- ½ tsp. salt-free mesquite seasoning
- 1 tbsp. pure maple syrup

Directions:

1. Line a baking sheet with parchment paper or a silicone mat.
2. Place the salmon onto the baking sheet (skin side down) and rub the seasoning evenly over each fillet. Drizzle the syrup onto the fillets, rubbing to coat the top.
3. Put the baking sheet in the oven and bake for 15 to 20 minutes.
4. Serve.

Nutrition:

- Calories: 223
- Total Fat: 9 g
- Carbs: 7 g
- Fiber: 0 g
- Protein: 28 g
- Calcium: 27 mg
- Sodium: 64 mg
- Potassium: 716 mg
- Vitamin D: 9 mcg
- Iron: 1 mg
- Zinc: 1 mg

Chapter 10
Salads

81. Southwest Corn and Black Bean Salad

Preparation Time: 10 minutes

Cooking Time: 0 minutes

Servings: 12

Ingredients:

- Black bean – 1 (15.5-ounce) can, low-Sodium: rinsed and drained
- Cooked corn – 1 cup
- Medium red onion – ½, chopped
- Medium tomato – 1, chopped
- Cucumber – ½, peeled and chopped
- Fresh cilantro – 2 Tbsp. minced
- 2 limes juice
- Extra-virgin olive oil – 1 Tbsp.
- Medium avocado – 1, pitted and diced
- Freshly ground black pepper to taste

Directions:

1. Combine corn, beans, onions, tomato, cucumber, and cilantro into a bowl.
2. Sprinkle with lime juice and toss to combine. Pour on olive oil and mix again.
3. Marinate in the refrigerator for at least 30 minutes.
4. Before serving, add avocado and season with pepper to taste.

Nutrition:

- Calories: 85
- Fat: 5g
- Carbs: 13 g
- Protein: 4g
- Sodium: 138 mg

82. Curried Chicken Salad

Preparation Time: 10 minutes

Cooking Time: 0 minutes

Servings: 4

Ingredients:

- Nonfat plain yogurt – ½ cup
- Curry powder – 1 tbsp.
- Cooked chicken – 2 cups, skinless, cut into bite-size pieces
- Medium apple – 1, peeled and diced
- Celery – 1 stalk, diced
- Dried cranberries – ½ cup
- Sesame seeds – ¼ cup, roasted and unsalted

Directions:

1. Combine yogurt, and curry powder in a bowl.
2. Add chicken, apple, celery, cranberries, and sesame seeds. Toss to combine.
3. Serve.

Nutrition:

- Calories: 259
- Fat: 6 g
- Carbs: 27 g
- Protein: 24 g
- Sodium: 230 mg

83. Chinese Chicken Salad

Preparation Time: 10 minutes

Cooking Time: 0 minutes

Servings: 2

Ingredients:

- Shredded Napa cabbage – 2 cups packed
- Roast chicken breast – 8 ounces, cut into ½-inch dice
- Large carrot – 1, shredded
- Medium red bell pepper – ½, cored and cut into thin strips
- Finely chopped fresh cilantro – 2 tbsp. plus more for sprinkling
- Vinaigrette from the couscous salad

Directions:

1. In a bowl, mix well the cabbage, chicken, carrot, bell pepper, and 2 tbsp. cilantro. Stir in the vinaigrette.
2. Sprinkle with additional cilantro and serve.

Nutrition:

- Calories: 335
- Fat: 20 g
- Carbs: 14 g
- Protein: 26 g
- Sodium: 760 mg

84. Turkey Salad with Apples and Dried Cranberries

Preparation Time: 10 minutes

Cooking Time: 0 minutes

Servings: 4

Ingredients:

- Buttermilk – ¼ cup
- Light mayonnaise - 2 Tbsp.
- Kosher salt – ¼ tsp.
- Freshly ground black pepper – ¼ tsp.
- Cooked turkey breast – 2 cups, cut into ½-inch dice
- Sweet apples – 2, cut into ½-inch dice
- Dried cranberries - ¼ cup
- Raw sunflower seeds – ¼ cup, unsalted
- Mixed salad greens – 5 cups

Directions:

1. In a bowl, whisk the mayonnaise, buttermilk, salt, and pepper.
2. Add the turkey, apples, cranberries, and sunflower seeds and mix well.
3. Divide the greens among four salad bowls.
4. Top each salad and serve.

Nutrition:

- Calories: 233
- Fat: 8 g
- Carbs: 22 g
- Protein: 20 g
- Sodium: 215 mg

85. Shrimp, Mango, and Black Bean Salad

Preparation Time: 10 minutes

Cooking Time: 5 minutes

Servings: 4

Ingredients:

- 2 tbsp. olive oil – plus olive oil cooking spray
- ¾ pound large shrimp, peeled and deveined
- 2 tbsp. fresh lime juice
- 2 ripe mangoes, cut into ½ inch dice
- 1 (15-ounce) can reduced-sodium black beans, drained and rinsed
- ½ jalapeno, seeded and rinsed
- 2 tbsp. finely chopped fresh cilantro or mint –
- 2 tbsp. minced red onion

Directions:

1. Spray a grill pan with oil.
2. Then and heat over medium heat.
3. Add the shrimp.

4. Cook for 3 to 5 minutes. Refrigerate to cool completely, about 20 minutes.
5. Whisk the lime juice and 2 tablespoons of oil in a bowl.
6. Add the shrimp, mango, beans, jalapeno, cilantro, and onion and toss gently.
7. Serve.

Nutrition:

- Calories: 213
- Fat: 2 g
- Carbs: 36 g
- Protein: 18 g
- Sodium: 679 mg

86. Tuna and Vegetable Salad

Preparation Time: 5 minutes

Servings: 2

Cooking Time: 0 minutes

Ingredients:

- 1 (5-ounce) can low-sodium tuna in water – drained
- 2 small celery ribs, finely diced
- 1 small carrot, shredded
- 1 small scallion, white part only, finely chopped
- 2 tbsp. light mayonnaise
- 2 tsp. fresh parsley or dill

Directions:

1. Mix everything in a bowl and serve.

Nutrition:

- Calories: 161
- Fat: 7 g
- Carbs: 6 g
- Protein: 18 g
- Sodium: 191 mg

87. Couscous Salad with Vinaigrette

Preparation Time: 10 minutes

Servings: 4

Cooking Time: 15 minutes

Ingredients:

- 1 ½ cups low sodium chicken broth
- 2 tbsp. olive oil – divided
- ¼ tsp. salt
- 1 ½ cups couscous
- ¼ cup orange juice
- 2 tbsp. white wine vinegar
- freshly ground black pepper
- 3 scallions, finely chopped
- 2 tbsp. fresh flat-leaf parsley – chopped
- 1/3 cup sliced almonds

Directions:

1. In a pot, add chicken broth and 1 tablespoon of olive oil. Bring to a boil.
2. Add couscous, stir, and cover. Remove from heat.
3. Let it sit for 5 minutes.
4. Then fluff with a fork.
5. Meanwhile, whisk together the remaining tablespoon of olive oil, orange juice, vinegar, ¼ tsp. salt, and black pepper in a bowl.
6. Pour vinaigrette over couscous and mix well.
7. Add in herbs, scallions, and sliced almonds.
8. Season with more pepper and serve.

Nutrition:

- Calories: 375
- Fat: 15 g
- Carbs: 52 g
- Protein: 9 g

- Sodium: 230 mg

88. California Cobb Salad

Preparation Time: 10 minutes

Servings: 4

Cooking Time: 0 minutes

Ingredients:

- 10 ounces baby spinach
- 2 tbsp. extra-virgin olive oil
- 1 ½ tbsp. lemon juice
- 3 slices low-sodium bacon – cooked
- 2 hard-boiled eggs – cut into bite-sized pieces
- 2 cups cooked chicken – skinless, cut into bite-size pieces
- 1 cup grape tomatoes – halved
- 2 avocados, pitted, cut into bite-sized pieces
- 1/3 cup blue cheese, crumbled
- freshly ground black pepper to taste

Directions:

1. In a bowl, toss spinach with olive oil and lemon juice.
2. Add bacon, eggs, chicken, tomatoes, avocado, and blue cheese. Toss to combine.
3. Season with pepper to taste and serve.

Nutrition:

- Calories: 450
- Fat: 34 g
- Carbs: 15 g
- Protein: 25 g
- Sodium: 450 mg

89. Chopped Greek Salad

Preparation Time: 10 minutes

Servings: 4

Cooking Time: 0 minutes

Ingredients:

- 1 small red onion, soaked for 30 minutes, then cut into very thin half-moons
- 1 tbsp. red wine vinegar
- 1 tbsp. water
- 1 tsp. dried oregano
- 1 clove garlic, minced
- 1/8 tsp. fresh ground black pepper
- 1 tbsp. extra-virgin olive oil
- 1 pint grape tomatoes, cut in halves
- 1 medium cucumber, peeled, seeded, and cut into thin half-moons
- ½ cup diced green bell pepper
- 2 ounces crumbled regular rindless goat cheese

Directions:

1. In a bowl, whisk the water, vinegar, oregano, garlic, and pepper.
2. Gradually whisk in the oil. Add the drained onion, tomatoes, cucumber, and bell pepper and toss well.
3. Sprinkle with goat cheese and serve.

Nutrition:

- Calories: 95
- Fat: 5 g
- Carbs: 10 g
- Protein: 5 g
- Sodium: 81 mg

90. Balsamic Beet Salad

Preparation Time: 5 minutes

Servings: 4

Cooking Time: 15 minutes

Ingredients:

- 6 medium-sized beets
- 1 cup water
- Kosher flavored vinegar

- Freshly ground black pepper
- Balsamic vinegar
- Extra virgin olive oil

Directions:

1. Wash the beets carefully and trim them to ½ inch portions. Add 1 cup of water to the pot.
2. Place a steamer/ trivet on top and arrange the beets on top of the steamer.
3. Lock up the lid and cook on HIGH pressure for 1 minute.
4. Release the pressure naturally and allow the beet to cool. Slice the top of the skin carefully.
5. Slice up the beets in uniform portions and season with flavored vinegar and pepper.
6. Add a splash of balsamic vinegar and allow them to marinate for 30 minutes.
7. Add a bit of extra olive oil and serve!

Nutrition:

- Calories: 120
- Fat: 7 g
- Carbs: 13 g
- Protein: 2 g

Chapter 11
Poultry

91. Thai Chicken Pasta

Preparation Time: 10 minutes

Cooking Time: 10 minutes

Servings: 6

- 6 oz. whole-wheat spaghetti, uncooked;
- 10 oz. sugar snap peas, trimmed and cut into strips;
- 1 cucumber, sliced;
- 2 cups carrots, julienned;
- 1 cup Thai peanut sauce;
- 2 tsp. canola oil;
- Fresh cilantro, chopped, for serving.

Ingredients:

- 2 cups chicken, cooked, shredded;

Directions:

1. Bring a saucepan of water to a boil and add pasta. Cook according to package instructions until al dente. Drain.
2. Preheat canola oil in a skillet over medium heat and add peas and carrots; cook for about 6-8 minutes.
3. Add cooked chicken, spaghetti, and peanut sauce. Toss well to combine, and cook for 1-2 minutes more.
4. Serve topped with fresh cilantro.

Nutrition:

- Calories: 192
- Fat: 5.3 g
- Carbs: 18.5 g
- Protein: 18.3 g
- Sodium: 120 mg
- Fiber: 3.6 g

92. Paprika Baked Chicken Breasts

Preparation Time: 10 minutes

Cooking Time: 30 minutes

Servings: 4-6

Ingredients:

- 4-6 chicken breasts, boneless;
- 1 tbsp. olive oil;
- 1 tbsp. paprika;
- 1/4 cup brown sugar;
- 1 tsp. ground coriander;
- 1/2 tsp. garlic powder;
- 1/4 tsp. cayenne pepper;
- 1/2 tsp. ground black pepper.

Directions:

1. Preheat the oven to 400°F. Prepare a baking sheet and line it with parchment paper.
2. Mix coriander, paprika, salt, sugar, black pepper, garlic powder, and cayenne pepper in a bowl.
3. Drizzle chicken breasts with oil and rub with the spice mixture and refrigerate for about 15 minutes.
4. Place on the baking sheet and cook for 30 minutes. Let cool before serving.

Nutrition:

- Calories: 349
- Fat: 14.6 g
- Carbs: 10.3 g
- Protein: 42.6 g
- Sodium: 129 mg
- Fiber: 0.8 g

93. Chicken Lettuce Wraps

Preparation Time: 10 minutes

Cooking Time: 10 minutes

Servings: 4

Ingredients:

- 8 lettuce leaves;
- 3/4 lb. chicken breasts, boneless, skinless, cubed;
- 1.5 cups carrots, shredded;
- 4 green onions, chopped;
- 1.25 cups fresh sweet cherries, pitted, chopped;
- 2 tsp. olive oil;
- 1/3 cup almonds, chopped;
- 2 tbsp. rice vinegar;
- 2 tbsp. low-sodium teriyaki sauce;
- 1 tbsp. honey;
- 1 tsp. ground ginger;
- 1/4 tsp. ground black pepper.

Directions:

1. Season chicken with ginger and pepper.
2. Preheat olive oil in a skillet over medium heat and add the chicken; cook for about 4-5 minutes until meat is no longer pink. Transfer to a plate.
3. Add carrots, green onions, almonds, and cherries to the same skillet. Stir well, and cook for 1-2 minutes. Add vinegar, honey, and teriyaki sauce. Add chicken and toss to combine.
4. Top each lettuce leaf with the chicken mixture and serve.

Nutrition:

- Calories: 257
- Fat: 10.2 g
- Carbs: 21.8 g
- Protein: 21.4 g
- Sodium: 181 mg
- Fiber: 4.0 g

94. Chicken Pita Sandwiches

Preparation Time: 1 hour

Cooking Time: 15 minutes

Servings: 4

Ingredients:

- 1 lb. chicken tenders
- 2 whole-wheat pita breads, halved
- 1 English cucumber, sliced
- 4 lettuce leaves
- 1/2 cup red onion, sliced
- 1 cup plum tomatoes, chopped
- 1 tbsp. fresh oregano, chopped
- 2 tsp. fresh mint, chopped
- 2 tsp. fresh dill, chopped
- 3/4 cup low-fat plain Greek yogurt
- 2 tbsp. lemon juice
- 1 tsp. lemon zest
- 5 tsp. olive oil
- 3 garlic cloves, minced
- 1/4 tsp. crushed red pepper
- 1 tsp. ground pepper

Directions:

1. Mix 3 tablespoons of olive oil, 2 garlic cloves, lemon zest, lemon juice, and red pepper in a bowl. Add chicken and toss well to coat, cover and refrigerate for at least 1 hour.
2. Mix dill, mint, yogurt, ground pepper, and the remaining oil and garlic in a bowl.
3. Preheat the grill to medium-high heat. Grease grilling gates with oil. Grill the chicken for 3-4 minutes per side.
4. Spread the yogurt sauce over pita bread and stuff with chicken mixture, lettuce, onion, tomatoes, and cucumbers.

Nutrition:

- Calories: 353
- Fat: 9.1 g
- Carbs: 33.1 g
- Protein: 37.2 g
- Sodium: 359 mg
- Fiber: 6.2 g

95. White Wine Garlic Chicken

Preparation Time: 10 minutes

Cooking Time: 25 minutes

Servings: 4

Ingredients:

- 4 chicken breast, boneless, skinless, pounded
- 6 oz. baby portobello mushrooms, sliced
- 1 onion, chopped
- 2 garlic cloves, minced
- 1/2 cup dry white wine
- 1 tbsp. olive oil
- 1/4 tsp. black pepper

Directions:

1. Season chicken with pepper.
2. Preheat olive oil in a skillet over medium heat. Add chicken and cook for about 6 minutes per side. Transfer to a plate.
3. Add onion and mushrooms to the same skillet, cook for 2-3 minutes.
4. Add garlic and cook for 1 minute.
5. Add wine and bring everything to a boil; stir well to combine everything. Cook for 1-2 minutes and serve.

Nutrition:

- Calories: 243
- Fat: 7.2 g
- Carbs: 5.1 g
- Protein: 36.3 g
- Sodium: 381 mg
- Fiber: 1.2 g

96. Turkey Medallions

Preparation Time: 30 minutes

Cooking Time: 15 minutes

Servings: 6

Ingredients:

- 20 oz. turkey tenderloins, sliced;
- 1 egg;
- 3 tbsp. olive oil;
- 2 tbsp. lemon juice;
- 1 cup panko breadcrumbs;
- 1/2 cup Parmesan cheese, grated;
- 1/2 cup walnuts, chopped;
- 1 tsp. lemon pepper seasoning;
- 1/4 tsp. pepper;
- Fresh basil, chopped.

Directions:

1. Mix egg and lemon juice in a bowl.
2. In a separate bowl, mix breadcrumbs, nuts, lemon pepper seasoning, and cheese.
3. Season turkey with pepper.
4. Preheat oil in a skillet over medium heat.
5. Dip each turkey piece first into the egg mixture and then into the breadcrumb mixture. Add to the skillet and cook for about 2-3 minutes per side. Serve topped with basil.

Nutrition:

- Calories: 351
- Fat: 21.2 g
- Carbs: 13.2 g
- Protein: 29.3 g
- Sodium: 458 mg
- Fiber: 2.2 g

97. Walnut Pesto Chicken Penne

Preparation Time: 20 minutes

Cooking Time: 30 minutes

Servings: 4

Ingredients:

- 1.5 cups chicken meat, cooked, shredded;
- 6 oz. whole-wheat penne pasta;
- 8 oz. green beans, trimmed and halved;
- 3/4 cup walnuts, chopped, toasted;
- 2 cups cauliflower florets;
- 1 cup fresh parsley leaves, chopped;
- 2 garlic cloves, crushed;
- 1/3 cup Parmesan cheese, grated;
- 2 tbsp. olive oil;
- A ground pepper pinch

Directions:

1. Bring a pot of water to a boil and add pasta and cook for about 4 minutes.
2. Add cauliflower and green beans, cook for 5-6 minutes more.
3. Mix walnuts, parsley, garlic, and pepper in a blender and blitz until the mixture is ground. Add Parmesan and process to combine. Mix chicken with the mixture.
4. Drain pasta with vegetables and top with cheese and chicken mixture. Toss well to combine and serve.

Nutrition:

- Calories: 514
- Fat: 27.4 g
- Carbs: 43.2 g
- Protein: 31.3 g
- Sodium: 457 mg
- Fiber: 9.2 g

98. Instant Pot Chicken Thighs with Olives and Capers

Preparation Time: 15 minutes

Cooking Time: 20 minutes

Servings: 6

Ingredients:

- 6 chicken thighs
- 3 tbsp. avocado oil
- ¼ tsp. sweet paprika
- A couple small lemons
- 1 cup chicken stock
- 1 cup pitted olives
- 3 tbsp. parsley leaves for garnish
- 1 tsp. kosher salt
- 1 tsp. ground turmeric
- ¼ tsp. black pepper
- ¼ tsp. mustard powder
- 2 tbsp. cooking fat of choice

- 2 chopped garlic cloves
- 2 tbsp. capers

Directions:
1. Season chicken thighs with salt and put them in a baking dish.
2. Mix together the spices with the avocado oil, put it over the chicken. Marinate for 20-30 minutes at room temperature.
3. Halve the lemons, and then heat the ghee, swirling to the pot bottom. Brown the chickens for 3 minutes undisturbed, and then brown the second side.
4. Do this with the rest of the chicken, and then use the broth to deglaze the pot.
5. Put lemons at the bottom and chicken over the top, and then the rest of the ingredients over the chicken.
6. Let it cook for 14 minutes.
7. When finished, let natural pressure release, and then taste to see if it's ready, and put olives and capers over the chicken, garnishing with parsley.

Nutrition:

- Calories: 253
- Fat: 6 g
- Carbs: 10 g
- Net Carbs: 6 g
- Protein: 13 g
- Fiber: 4 g

99. Instant pot Mediterranean Chicken

Preparation Time: 15 minutes

Cooking Time: 5 minutes

Servings: 8

Ingredients:

- 8-10 organic, boneless, and skinless chicken thighs
- 1 tsp. paprika
- ¼ tsp. chili powder
- 2 tsp. dried parsley
- Salt and pepper for taste
- ½ cup black olives
- 2 tbsp. olive oil
- 1 tsp. onion powder
- ½ tsp. coriander seed, ground
- 2 tsp. dried oregano
- 1 can of dried and chopped tomatoes

Directions:
1. Set your IP to sauté, and then add the olive oil to the bottom to heat.
2. Add chicken and sauté until it's browned but not cooked.
3. Add onions, cook for 5 minutes, and add all spices, tomatoes, salt, pepper, and cook for 3 minutes.
4. Put the chicken back in, combine it together, manual cook for 8 minutes, and then let it naturally steam release, then put the black olives in to stir.
5. It can be served best over pasta, rice, veggies, or mashed potatoes, and cauliflower.

Nutrition:

- Calories: 153
- Fat: 8 g
- Carbs: 9 g
- Net Carbs: 7 g
- Protein: 12 g
- Fiber: 2 g

100. Green Chicken and Rice Bowl

Preparation Time: 10 minutes

Cooking Time: 32 minutes

Servings: 4

Ingredients:

- 1 cup chicken broth
- 3 cups water

- ½ tsp. cumin, paprika, thyme, and turmeric
- 4 tbsp. hummus
- ½ cup Kalamata olives
- 2 chicken breasts, skinless
- 2 cups basmati rice
- ½ tsp. red pepper
- salt and pepper for taste
- 4 tbsp. tzatziki sauce
- 4 tbsp. feta cheese

Directions:
1. Season chicken with spices.
2. Add chicken to instant pot with the broth.
3. Cook on manual high pressure, then release naturally for 10 minutes.
4. Remove chicken and then shred chicken.
5. Rinse rice and then add it to the instant pot, cooking for 22 minutes on high pressure, then natural pressure release.
6. Add the rice, chicken, and the rest of the ingredients to make a rice bowl.

Nutrition:
- Calories: 426
- Fat: 10 g
- Carbs: 12 g
- Net Carbs: 5 g
- Protein: 25 g
- Fiber: 7 g

Chapter 12
Snacks

101. Avocado Wedges

Preparation: 5 minutes

Cooking Time: 10 minutes

Servings: 4

Ingredients:

- 2 avocados, peeled, pitted, and cut into wedges
- 1 tbsp. avocado oil
- 1 tbsp. lime juice
- 1 tsp. coriander, ground

Directions:

1. Spread the avocado wedges on a lined baking sheet, add oil and other ingredients. Toss, and bake at 300°F for 10 minutes.
2. Divide into cups and serve as a snack.

Nutrition:

- Calories: 212
- Fat: 20.1 g
- Fiber: 6.9 g
- Carbs: 9.8 g
- Protein: 2 g

102. Lemon Dip

Preparation: 4 minutes

Cooking Time: 0 minutes

Servings: 4

- 1 cup low-fat cream cheese
- Black pepper to the taste
- ½ cup lemon juice
- 1 tbsp. cilantro, chopped
- 3 garlic cloves, chopped

Ingredients:

Directions:

1. Mix the cream cheese with the lemon juice and the other ingredients in your food processor, pulse well, and divide into bowls and serve.

Nutrition:

- Calories: 213
- Fat: 20.5 g
- Fiber: 0.2 g
- Carbs: 2.8 g
- Protein: 4.8 g

103. Sweet Potato Dip

Preparation Time: 10 minutes

Cooking Time: 40 minutes

Ingredients:

Servings: 4

- 1 cup sweet potatoes, peeled and cubed

- 1 tbsp. low-sodium veggie stock
- Cooking spray
- 2 tbsp. coconut cream
- 2 tsp. Rosemary, dried
- Black pepper to the taste

Directions:

1. In a baking pan, combine the potatoes with the stock and the other ingredients. Stir, bake at 365°F for 40 minutes. Transfer to your blender, pulse well, divide into small bowls and serve

Nutrition:

- Calories: 65
- Fat: 2.1 g
- Fiber: 2 g
- Carbs: 11.3 g
- Protein: 0.8 g

104. Beans Salsa

Preparation Time: 5 minutes

Cooking Time: 0 minutes

Servings: 4

Ingredients:

- 1 cup canned black beans, no-salt-added, drained
- 1 cup canned red kidney beans, no-salt-added, drained
- 1 tsp. balsamic vinegar
- 1 cup cherry tomatoes, cubed
- 1 tbsp. olive oil
- 2 shallots, chopped

Directions:

1. In a bowl, combine the beans with the vinegar and the other ingredients. Toss, and serve as a party snack.

Nutrition:

- Calories: 362
- Fat: 4.8 g
- Fiber: 14.9 g
- Carbs: 61 g
- Protein: 21.4 g

105. Green Beans Salsa

Preparation Time: 10 minutes

Cooking Time: 10 minutes

Servings: 4

Ingredients:

- 1-pound green beans, trimmed and halved
- 1 tbsp. olive oil
- 2 tsp. capers, drained
- 6 ounces green olives, pitted and sliced
- 4 garlic cloves, minced
- 1 tbsp. lime juice
- 1 tbsp. oregano, chopped
- Black pepper to the taste

Directions:

1. Heat oil to a pot over medium heat. Add garlic and green beans, mix well and cook for 3 minutes.
2. Add all the ingredients, toss, cook for another 7 minutes, divide into small cups and serve cold.

Nutrition:

- Calories: 111
- Fat: 6.7 g
- Fiber: 5.6 g
- Carbs: 13.2 g
- Protein: 2.9 g

106. Delicious Berry Pie

Preparation Time: 10 minutes
Cooking Time: 1 hour

Servings: 6

Ingredients:

- ½ cup whole wheat flour
- Cooking spray
- 1/3 cup almond milk
- ¼ tsp. baking powder
- ¼ tsp. stevia
- ¼ cup blueberries
- 1 tsp. olive oil
- 1 tsp. vanilla extract
- ½ tsp. lemon zest, grated

Directions:

1. In a bowl, mix flour with baking powder, stevia, blueberries, milk, oil, lemon zest, vanilla extract and whisk. Pour into your slow cooker lined with parchment paper, and grease with the cooking spray. Cover, and cook on High for 1 hour.
2. Leave the pie to cool down, slice, and serve.

Nutrition:

- Calories: 82
- Fat: 4.2 g
- Cholesterol: 0 mg
- Sodium: 3m g
- Carbs: 10.1 g
- Fiber: 0.7 g
- Sugars: 1.2 g
- Protein: 1.4 g
- Potassium: 74 mg

107. Carrot Spread

Preparation Time: 10 minutes
Cooking Time: 30 minutes

Servings: 4

Ingredients:

- 1-pound carrots, peeled and chopped
- ½ cup walnuts, chopped
- 2 cups low-sodium veggie stock
- 1 cup coconut cream
- 1 tbsp. rosemary, chopped
- 1 tsp. garlic powder
- ¼ tsp. smoked paprika

Directions:

1. In a small pot, mix the carrots with the stock, walnuts, and the other ingredients except for the cream and the rosemary. Stir, bring to a boil over medium heat, cook for 30 minutes, drain and transfer to a blender.
2. Add the cream, blend the mix well. Divide into bowls, sprinkle the rosemary on top, and serve.

Nutrition:

- Calories: 201
- Fat: 8.7 g
- Fiber: 3.4 g
- Carbs: 7.8 g
- Protein: 7.7 g

108. Tomato Dip

Preparation Time: 10 minutes
Cooking Time: 10 minutes

Servings: 4

Ingredients:

- 1-pound tomatoes, peeled and chopped
- ½ cup garlic, minced
- 2 tbsp. olive oil
- A black pepper pinch
- 2 shallots, chopped

- 1 tsp. thyme, dried

Directions:

1. Heat oil in a pan over medium heat, add garlic and shallots. Stir and fry for 2 minutes.
2. Add the tomatoes and the other ingredients, cook for 8 minutes more and transfer to a blender.
3. Pulse well, divide into small cups, and serve as a snack.

Nutrition:

- Calories: 232
- Fat: 11.3g
- Fiber: 3.9 g
- Carbs: 7.9 g
- Protein: 4.5 g

109. Salmon Bowls

Preparation Time: 10 minutes

Cooking Time: 0 minutes

Servings: 6

Ingredients:

- 1 tbsp. avocado oil
- 1 tbsp. balsamic vinegar
- ½ tsp. oregano, dried
- 1 cup smoked salmon, no-salt-added, boneless, skinless, and cubed
- 1 cup salsa
- 4 cups baby spinach

Directions:

1. In a bowl, combine the salmon with the salsa and the other ingredients. Toss, divide into small cups and serve.

Nutrition:

- Calories: 281
- Fat: 14.4 g
- Fiber: 7.4 g
- Carbs: 18.7 g
- Protein: 7.4 g

110. Tomato and Corn Salsa

Preparation Time: 4 minutes

Cooking Time: 0 minutes

Servings: 4

Ingredients:

- 3 cups corn
- 2 cups tomatoes, cubed
- 2 green onions, chopped
- 2 tbsp. olive oil
- 1 red chili pepper, chopped
- ½ tbsp. chives, chopped

Directions:

1. In a salad bowl, combine the tomatoes with the corn and the other ingredients. Toss, and serve cold as a snack.

Nutrition:

- Calories: 178
- Fat: 8.6 g
- Fiber: 4.5 g
- Carbs: 25.9 g
- Protein: 4.7 g

Chapter 13
Dressings, Sauces & Condiments

111. Avocado Dressing

Preparation Time: 3 minutes

Cooking Time: 2 minutes

Servings: 4

Ingredients:

- Three-fourths tbsp. lemon juice
- 4 oz. olive oil
- 8 oz. avocado
- One/eight tsp. garlic powder
- One-third cup water

Directions:

1. Remove the skin from the avocado and transfer it to a food blender.
2. Combine the lemon juice, garlic powder, water, and olive oil to the blender. Pulse for approximately 45 seconds well mixed.
3. Keep in a jar or lidded tub in the fridge for up to 7 days.

Nutrition:

- Calories: 299
- Sodium: 27 mg
- Protein: 1 g
- Fat: 33 g
- Sugar: 0 g

112. Barbeque Sauce

Preparation Time: 50 minutes

Cooking Time: 40 minutes

Servings: 4

Ingredients:

- Two-thirds tsp. black pepper
- One tsp. lemon juice
- Two-thirds cup tomato sauce, salt-free (See Helpful Tip below)
- One-third cup water
- Two and two-thirds tbsp. brown sugar
- One and two-thirds tbsp. sugar, granulated
- Two-thirds tsp. ground mustard
- One-third cup apple cider vinegar
- One tsp. Worcestershire sauce, low-sodium
- Two-thirds tsp. onion powder

Directions:

1. In a saucepan, blend the tomato sauce, apple cider vinegar, brown sugar, granulated sugar, and water.
2. Season with pepper, lemon juice, onion powder, mustard, and Worchester shire sauce.
3. Heat the mixture to a slow bubble and turn the temperature of the burner down to the lowest setting.
4. Cover the saucepan and heat for approximately 60 minutes as the sauce reduces.
5. Take the sauce away from the burner and let it rest for a minimum of half an hour before storing it in a lidded jar or tub.

Nutrition:

- Calories: 48
- Sodium: 38 mg
- Protein: 0 g
- Fat: 0 g
- Sugar: 11 g

113. Chicken Broth

Preparation Time: 1 hour

Cooking Time: 1 hour 15 minutes

Servings: 4

Ingredients:

- One roasted chicken carcass
- Water
- One cup vegetable trimming, chopped roughly
- Three tbsp. white vinegar

Directions:

1. Use a deep pot to place the chicken carcasses, vinegar, and vegetable scraps.
2. Cover the chicken fully with water and heat until bubbling.
3. Turn the burner down and allow to simmer for approximately 2 hours as the broth reduces.
4. Remove the solid materials with a slotted spoon or tongs. You may also use a fine-mesh strainer if you want purer broth.
5. Place the turkey breast slice on a plate and cover it with a thin layer of cream cheese.
6. Transfer to ziplock bags or a lidded tub to store in the freezer for up to a month or can be used immediately.

Nutrition:

- Calories: 8
- Sodium: 42 mg
- Protein: 0 g
- Fat: 0 g
- Sugar: 0 g

114. French Dressing

Preparation: 3 minutes

Cooking Time: 2 minutes

Servings: 4

Ingredients:

- One/eight cup vinegar, white wine
- One-third tsp. mustard (See Helpful Tip below)
- One/eight cup olive oil
- One-third tsp. tomato paste, low-sodium (See Helpful Tip below)
- One/eight tsp. onion powder
- One-third tsp. honey

Directions:

1. Use a food blender to pulse the mustard, onion powder, tomato paste, olive oil, honey, and vinegar for approximately half a minute.
2. Remove to a lidded tub or Mason jar to store in the fridge. It will keep for about two weeks.

Nutrition:

- Calories: 56
- Sodium: 17 mg
- Protein: 0 g
- Fat: 6 g
- Sugar: 2 g

115. Italian Dressing

Preparation: 3 minutes

Cooking Time: 2 minutes

Servings: 4

Ingredients:

- One tsp. sugar, granulated
- Two oz. olive oil
- One oz. vinegar, white wine
- One and one-half tbsp. water
- One tsp. basil seasoning
- Three-fourths tsp. Mrs. Dash's seasoning mix
- One-half tbsp. mayonnaise, low-sodium (See Helpful Tip below)
- One-fourth tsp. garlic powder

Directions:

1. Use a food blender to pulse the vinegar, olive oil, mayonnaise, sugar, and water for about 15 seconds.
2. Combine the garlic powder, basil, and Mrs. Dash into the blender and pulse for an additional 30 seconds until smooth.
3. Transfer to a glass container or tub that has a cover and refrigerate for 5 days until needed.

Nutrition:

- Calories: 119
- Sodium: 14 mg
- Protein: 0 g
- Fat: 13 g
- Sugar: 1 g

116. Marinara Sauce

Preparation: 40 minutes

Servings: 4

Cooking Time: 35 minutes

Ingredients:

- Three-fourths tbsp. sugar, granulated
- One/eight cup onions, chopped
- 8 oz. can tomato sauce, salt-free (See Helpful Tip below)
- Three-fourths tbsp. ground oregano seasoning
- 4 tbsp. tomato paste, salt-free (See Helpful Tip below)
- One and one-half tbsp. garlic, minced
- Olive oil cooking spray
- One tbsp. basil seasoning
- Three-fourths cups water
- One/eight tsp. red pepper flakes, crushed

Directions:

1. Remove the outer skin from the onion and chop into small cubes.
2. Coat a skillet with the olive oil spray, empty the onions, and brown for approximately 5 minutes.
3. Blend the water, tomato paste, and sauce into the frying pan and toss to completely coat the onions.
4. Season with the oregano, garlic, sugar, basil, and red pepper flakes and blend until combined.
5. Turn the burner to low and simmer for approximately half an hour.
6. Take away from the burner and cool for another half hour before storing.

Nutrition:

- Calories: 52
- Sodium: 21 mg
- Protein: 2 g
- Fat: 0 g
- Sugar: 7 g

117. Peanut Butter

Preparation: 2 minutes

Servings: 4

Cooking Time: 8 minutes

Ingredients:

- One/eight tsp. salt
- One cup roasted peanuts, unsalted
- Two tsp. sugar, granulated
- One-fourth tbsp. olive oil

Directions:

1. Use a food blender to pulse the olive oil, roasted peanuts, sugar, and salt together for approximately 10 minutes.
2. Use a rubber scraper to remove the peanut butter from the sides of the dish as needed as it becomes smoother.
3. Transfer to a mason jar or a tub with a cover and keep fresh in the refrigerator for up to one month.

Nutrition:

- Calories: 190
- Sodium: 18 mg
- Protein: 16 g
- Fat: 7 g
- Sugar: 2 g

118. Ranch Dressing

Preparation: 3 minutes

Cooking Time: 2 minutes

Ingredients:

- One/eight cup sour cream, fat-free
- One-fourth cup buttermilk, low-fat
- One/eight tsp. black pepper
- One-fourth tbsp. dill weed, chopped

Servings: 8

- One/eight tsp. garlic powder
- One-fourth tbsp. parsley, chopped
- One-fourth tbsp. mustard, low-sodium (See Helpful Tip below)
- One-fourth tsp. onion powder

Directions:

1. Use a big glass dish to blend the buttermilk, sour cream, and mustard until integrated.
2. Season with the dill weed, pepper, parsley, garlic powder, and onion powder until combined.
3. Transfer to a glass jar or lidded tub to store in the refrigerator for up to 7 days.

Nutrition:

- Calories: 8
- Sodium: 17 mg
- Protein: 0 g
- Fat: 0 g
- Sugar: 1 g

119. Soy Sauce

Preparation: 35 minutes

Cooking Time: 35 minutes

Ingredients:

- Two tsp. brown sugar
- One tsp. vinegar, balsamic
- Two tbsp. vegetable broth, low-salt
- One-fourth tsp. black pepper

Servings: 4

- One tsp. sesame oil
- One/eight tsp. garlic powder
- Three tsp. vinegar, red wine
- Two oz. water

Directions:

1. Warm the water in a saucepan until it is bubbling. Turn the burner off.
2. Blend the vinegars, vegetable broth, sesame oil, garlic powder, brown sugar, and pepper and fully combine.
3. Wait approximately 60 minutes before serving.

Nutrition:

- Calories: 23
- Sodium: 25 mg
- Protein: 0 g
- Fat: 1 g
- Sugar: 0 g

120. Tartar Sauce

Preparation: 3 minutes

Cooking Time: 2 minutes

Servings: 10

Ingredients:

- One-half cup mayonnaise, low-sodium (See Helpful Tip below)
- Three tsp. onion, minced
- One-half tsp. lemon juice
- One and one-half tsp. sugar, granulated
- Three tsp. sweet relish, low-sodium

Directions:

1. Use a food blender to pulse the sugar, mayonnaise, lemon juice, onion and relish for approximately half a minute until incorporated.
2. Transfer into a lidded tub or Mason jar and keep fresh in the fridge for 7 days.

Nutrition:

- Calories: 33
- Sodium: 59 mg
- Protein: 0 g
- Fat: 3 g
- Sugar: 0 g

Conclusion

Unlike the regular diets out there, DASH is a tad bit different. It stands for "Dietary Approaches to Stop Hypertension." Yes, you read that right. Finally, a diet that focuses on one of the greatest killers of the 21st century— hypertension. According to recent studies, one out of three adults suffers from hypertension or high blood pressure. It keeps increasing with age, with almost two-thirds of the population suffering from it from the age of 65. High blood pressure is not a single stroke disease— it brings heart trouble, kidney diseases, and even diabetes.

The diet also has many health benefits as it helps reduce hypertension and obesity, lower osteoporosis, and prevent cancer. This well-balanced diet strengthens metabolism, which further helps in decomposing the fat deposits stored in the body. As a result, it improves and enhances the overall health of a person.

This cookbook has provided you different Dash meals from breakfast, lunch, dinner, mains, side dishes, fish and seafood, poultry, vegetables, soups, salads, snacks, and desserts. However, you can consult experts if you suffer from current health conditions or follow certain exercise routines, as this will help you customize the diet as per your requirement.

This diet is easy to follow as you get to everything but in a healthier fashion and limited quantity. Talking about the DASH diet outside the theory and more in practice reveals its efficiency as a diet. Besides excess research and experiments, the real reasons for people looking into this diet are its specific features. It gives the feeling of ease and convenience, making the users more comfortable with its rules and regulations.

The Dash Diet Cookbook will have you hacking out your cutlery in no time so you can finally become a healthier human being! It's all about being healthy and learning to enjoy the foods you eat again. We have concluded that Dash Diet Cookbook is an excellent way of losing weight and following a healthy, balanced diet. The Dash Diet Cookbook is a collection of simple recipes that are easy to prepare and incredibly tasty. Many different styles of cooking are featured, so you can find something that works for you. The Dash Diet Cookbook is perfect for anyone who wants to eat better and feel great while saving money and time.

When research into diet plans for hypertension began, they did not focus too much on weight loss. They were more concerned with getting the blood pressure levels regulated. But soon, the researchers realized that healthy weight loss was the need of the hour, and therefore there were an additional need to create a systematic weight loss plan and reduced blood pressure levels. So, after a lot of deliberation, the DASH diet for weight loss was also formulated, including nuts, cereals, whole fruits and vegetables, and seeds.

Unlike other flyby diets, which are more word of mouth than scientific, the DASH diet is primarily based on scientific principles of good health. The research on DASH diets indicates that it is not merely a tool for reducing your blood pressure by eating a low sodium diet. The plan is designed for each person, keeping their specific needs in mind. It comprises wholesome foods, such as fruits, vegetables, grains, fresh produce, etc. which keeps the body in fighting fit condition. Top rung research institutes such as the American Heart Association, Dietary Guidelines for Americans, the National Heart, Lung, and Blood Institute- all endorse this diet plan.

Several more corroborating research reports later, the DASH diet was further improved to optimize health and reduce hypertension by increasing protein intake and cutting down on empty carbs and bad fats. The DASH diet's basic premise is based on sound scientific principles of attainable and sustainable weight loss. The meals and snacks prescribed in the diet plan comprise Fat: fibrous foods, which keep you filled for hours and do not let you snack mindlessly. They are designed to keep your blood sugar levels regulated instead of the spike and crash cycles, as seen with other diets. By following this diet, you keep your blood sugar levels on an even keel, defeat other diseases like diabetes, reduce your triglycerides, melt your stubborn belly Fat: lower your LDL, improve your HDL numbers, and generally feel healthier on average. Of course, a significant portion of the diet is protein-rich, so you build your muscle and lose body Fat. In the process, you avoid slowing your metabolism, which aids in sustaining your current weight.

Even if you are not suffering from hypertension, you can adopt the DASH diet to keep your internal systems healthy and robust.

Index

B

Baking Powder Biscuits; 3; 13

C

Creamy Oats, Greens & Blueberry Smoothie; 3; 14

.

. Apples and Fennel Mix; 4; 26

"

"Split" Pea and Sundried Tomatoes Soup; 5; 49

A

Almond Butter Pork Chops; 5; 43

Angel Hair with Smoked Salmon & Asparagus; 6; 57

Avocado Cup with Egg; 3; 17

Avocado Dressing; 7; 76

Avocado Wedges; 7; 71

B

Baked Haddock with Peppers & Eggplant; 6; 53

Baking Powder Biscuits; 3; 14

Balsamic Beet Salad; 6; 63

Barbeque Sauce; 7; 76

Bass with Citrus Butter; 6; 57

Beans Salsa; 7; 72

Beef Soup; 5; 43

Broccoli with Garlic and Lemon; 4; 32

Brown-Rice Pilaf; 4; 33

C

Cabbage and Leek Soup; 5; 51

F

Flaxseed & Banana Smoothie; 3; 14

O

Oatmeal Banana Pancakes with Walnuts; 3; 13

Cabbage Slaw; 4; 29

California Cobb Salad; 6; 63

Carrot Slaw; 4; 28

Carrot Spread; 7; 73

Carrot-Cake Smoothie; 4; 35

Cauliflower Mashed "Potatoes"; 4; 31

Cereal with Cranberry-Orange Twist; 3; 16

Chicken Broth; 7; 76

Chicken Lettuce Wraps; 6; 66

Chicken Pita Sandwiches; 7; 66

Chickpea Burgers; 3; 22

Chinese Chicken Salad; 6; 61

Chopped Greek Salad; 6; 63

Chunky Black-Bean Dip; 4; 33

Cinnamon Ice Cream; 4; 38

Classic Hummus; 4; 34

Cool Cabbage Fried Beef; 5; 45

Couscous Salad with Vinaigrette; 6; 62

Crazy Japanese Potato and Beef Croquettes; 5; 45

Creamy Oats, Greens & Blueberry Smoothie; 3; 15

Crispy Potato Skins; 4; 34

Curried Chicken Salad; 6; 60

Curried Kabocha Squash Soup; 5; 47

D

Decent Beef and Onion Stew; 5; 42

Delicious Berry Pie; 7; 73

E

Elegant Cranberry Muffins; 4; 37

F

Flaxseed & Banana Smoothie; 3; 15

French Dressing; 7; 77

Fruity Tofu Smoothie; 3; 15

G

Green Chicken and Rice Bowl; 7; 69

H

Healthy Avocado Beef Patties; 5; 44

Healthy Berry Cobbler; 5; 40

Hearty Cashew and Almond butter; 4; 37

Hearty Pineapple Pudding; 5; 40

Hearty Pork Belly Casserole; 5; 43

Herbed Mushroom Rice; 3; 22

House's Special Cashew Spring Green Soup; 5; 49

I

Instant Pot Chicken Thighs with Olives and Capers; 7; 68

Instant pot Mediterranean Chicken; 7; 69

Italian Dressing; 7; 77

K

Kale and Potato Soup Straight From Ireland; 5; 47

L

Lemon Dip; 7; 71

M

Maple-Glazed Salmon; 6; 59

Marinara Sauce; 7; 78

Marinated Lime Grilled Shrimp; 6; 55

Mesmerizing Avocado and Chocolate Pudding; 5; 39

Meticulous Butternut Squash Soup; 5; 48

Mexican Beans and Rice; 3; 24

N

No-Cook Overnight Oats; 3; 16

O

Oatmeal Banana Pancakes with Walnuts; 3; 14

Omnipotent Organic Chicken Thigh Soup; 5; 50

P

Paprika Baked Chicken Breasts; 6; 65

Pasta Primavera; 3; 20

Peanut Butter; 7; 78

Penne with White Beans and Roasted Tomato Sauce; 3; 21

Pork, White Bean, and Spinach Soup; 5; 46

Potato and Carrot "Impeccable" Soup; 5; 48

Q

Quinoa and Lentil Soup; 5; 51

R

Ranch Dressing; 7; 78

Ravaging Beef Pot Roast; 5; 44

Red Lentil Stew; 3; 20

Roasted Brussels Sprouts; 4; 32

Roasted Chickpeas; 4; 35

S

Salmon Bowls; 7; 74

Saucy Penne with Shrimp, Peas & Walnuts; 6; 56

Seared Mahi-Mahi with Lemon & Parsley; 6; 58

Shrimp & Broccoli with Angel Hair; 6; 55

Shrimp, Mango, and Black Bean Salad; 6; 61

Simple Roasted Celery Mix; 4; 27

Southwest Corn and Black Bean Salad; 6; 60

Southwestern Bean-And-Pepper Salad; 4; 31

Soy Sauce; 8; 79

Spicy Bean Chili; 3; 23

Spinach, Egg, and Cheese Breakfast Quesadillas; 3; 18

Sprouts Side Salad; 4; 28

Squash Salsa; 4; 26

Stylish Chocolate Parfait; 4; 39

Supreme Matcha Bomb; 5; 39

Sweet Potato Dip; 7; 71

Sweet Potatoes with Coconut Flakes; 3; 17

T

Tartar Sauce; 8; 79

Tasty Poached Apples; 5; 41

Tex-Mex Cod with Roasted Peppers & Corn; 6; 54

Thai Chicken Pasta; 6; 65

The Refreshing Nutter; 4; 37

Thyme Spring Onions; 4; 27

Tilapia Tacos with Chipotle Cream; 6; 53

Tofu Scramble with Potatoes and Mushrooms; 3; 23

Tomato and Corn Salsa; 7; 74

Tomato Dip; 7; 73

Tomato-Avocado Soup; 3; 19

Tomatoes Side Salad; 4; 26

Tuna and Vegetable Salad; 6; 62

Turkey Medallions; 7; 67

Turkey Salad with Apples and Dried Cranberries; 6; 61

V

Very Low Carb Ham and Cabbage Bowl; 5; 50

W

Walnut Pesto Chicken Penne; 7; 68

Watermelon Tomato Salsa; 4; 28

White Bean and Roasted Red Pepper Soup; 3; 19

White Wine Garlic Chicken; 7; 67

Z

Zucchini and Brussels Sprouts Salad; 4; 29

Zucchini Beef Sauté with Coriander Greens; 5; 42

Made in the USA
Monee, IL
26 March 2023

30562587R00046